Germany In The Later Middle Ages 1200 1500

William Stubbs

GERMANY IN THE LATER
MIDDLE AGES

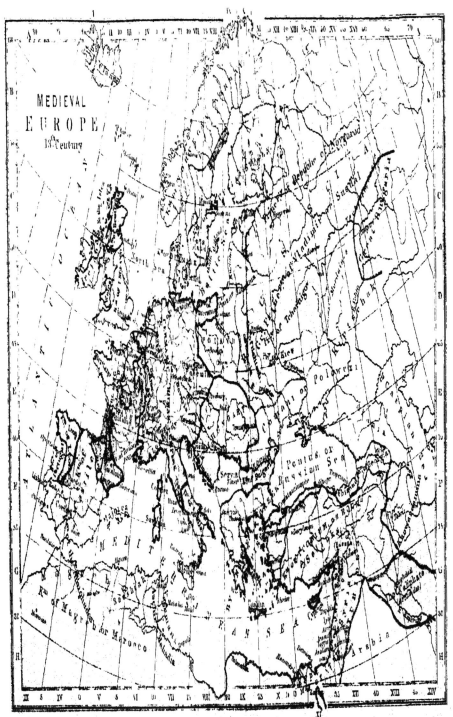

MEDIEVAL
EUROPE
13th Century

Longmans Green & Co. London, New York, Bombay & Calcutta

GERMANY IN THE LATER MIDDLE AGES, 1200–1500

BY WILLIAM STUBBS, D.D., FORMERLY BISHOP OF OXFORD, AND REGIUS PROFESSOR OF MODERN HISTORY IN THE UNIVERSITY OF OXFORD

EDITED BY

ARTHUR HASSALL, M.A.

STUDENT, TUTOR, AND SOMETIME CENSOR OF CHRIST CHURCH, OXFORD

LONGMANS, GREEN AND CO.

39 PATERNOSTER ROW, LONDON

NEW YORK, BOMBAY, AND CALCUTTA

1908

PREFATORY NOTE

THIS volume completes the series of Lectures given by
Bishop Stubbs on Germany in the Middle Ages. A
previous volume dealt with the history of Germany
from 476 A.D. to the middle of the thirteenth century;
the present volume carries on that history to the close
of the fifteenth century.

While the earlier volume was concerned especially
with the characters and careers of the Emperors in the
Dark Ages, the present volume follows the history of
Germany in a more detailed fashion, and may be described as a storehouse of facts and generalisations.

No such history of Germany in the English language
exists, and it may confidently be assumed that the appearance of this volume will be received with immense
pleasure by all students of the History of Europe in the
Middle Ages.

The thirteenth, fourteenth, and fifteenth centuries
present to the student of European history difficulties
of no ordinary kind. The period which marks the transition from the Middle Ages to modern times, and which
saw the rapid break-up of a Christendom which had
for its centre the Holy Roman Empire, and in its place
the gradual formation of the modern European States-
system, requires for its elucidation a close acquaintance
with the history of Medieval Europe.

No English historian has yet appeared who was so
eminently qualified to undertake the task of describing

the history of Germany and indeed of Europe during
this period of transition as was Bishop Stubbs. In the
present as in the previous volume the character-sketches
are the work of a master hand, while the account of the
institutions and constitution of Germany will enable
the historical student to follow and to comprehend the
peculiar and exceptional developments which took place
in the Holy Roman Empire.

ARTHUR HASSALL.

CONTENTS

CHAPTER I

CHAPTER II

CHAPTER III

CHAPTER IV

CHAPTER V

CHAPTER VI

CHAPTER VII

CHAPTER VIII

CHAPTER IX

CHAPTER X

CHAPTER XI

CHAPTER XII

MAPS

SOME AUTHORITIES

JOINVILLE : Vie de Saint Louis.
PHILIPPE DE COMMINES Mémoires.

LAVISSE ET RAMBAUD : Histoire Générale.
MILMAN : Latin Christianity.
GIBBON : The Decline and Fall (Bury's Edition).
COXE : House of Austria.
CAMBRIDGE MODERN HISTORY, Vol. I.
LAVISSE : Histoire de France.
KITCHIN : History of France, Vols I. and II.
RAMBAUD : Histoire de la Civilisation en France.
CREIGHTON : History of the Papacy.
ARMSTRONG : Lorenzo de' Medici.
BLOK : History of the People of the Netherlands (Translated).
HALLAM : Middle Ages.
TOUT : The Empire and the Papacy.
LODGE : The Close of the Middle Ages.

HISTORICAL MAPS, ed. Poole (Clarendon Press).
CHRONOLOGY : Hassall, " A Handbook of European History Chrono-
    logically Arranged."

GERMANY IN THE LATER MIDDLE AGES

1200-1500

CHAPTER I

Summary of results arrived at—Germany in the twelfth century—The chief points in its history between 1200 and 1600—The Empire and the Papacy—The death of Frederick Barbarossa an epoch in German history.

The Object of this Book.—My intention in this work is not to treat the history of Germany so much in its imperial as in its national aspect, and that intention will be carried out as rigorously as possible by the exclusion of all imperial questions which do not touch German life and nationality, such as all minute investigations into the imperial policy in Italy, and the antagonism outside of Germany between the imperial and papal ideas. This plan I have attempted hitherto to pursue, even at periods at which the personal history of the popes and emperors was most closely interwoven; and it ought not to be less easy to do so in periods like that to which we are coming, in which the Italian campaigns of the emperors became few and far between, and their influence upon the papacy was being quickly reduced to a shadow of what it had been.

But, in general, I am not one of those who think that all the interest of a national history necessarily

A

centres about the personal adventures of its rulers. To a certain extent it is so, but simply because the ancient writers to whom we are indebted for nearly all the details of the events of these ages have so treated history, possessing, indeed, by force of circumstances, so limited a field of view that they were obliged, if they would record anything at all, to record the actions mainly of kings and princes. But, true as this is, it is a truth which it is easy to exaggerate; for even the most courtly of historians, the most devoted of biographers preserves some particulars showing the real under-current of national history, and besides the biographers we have large quantities of legal and other documents which are of far wider than mere antiquarian interest.

From a comparison of such remains it is possible to get a notion of national life and development, separated from the mere adventures of kings, and from the noise and tumult of wars, and the minute investigations of births, deaths, and marriages. Well, in pursuance of some such idea, we have, in the preceding volume,[1] read the history of Germany down to the reign of Frederick II., and the following are some of the results that we have reached, such as it is necessary to recapitulate for our guidance, and for the connection of the history of the period to which we are now come.

Recapitulation.—We began by tracing very briefly the movements of the different nations of Germany to the period at which modern history may be said to begin, at the commencement of which the movements ceased and the lines of demarcation between the several tribal families which constitute the Germany of the Middle Ages permanently fix themselves. We traced and

[1] "Germany in the Early Middle Ages."

accounted for the limits and the divisions between the five nations—the Franks, the Alemanni, the Saxons, the Bavarians, and the Lotharingians. Of these we saw that the Bavarians were the only nation that could, strictly speaking, be called a distinct nation; the Saxons, Franks, and Alemanni being rather associations of separate tribes, and the Lotharingians the inhabitants of a district variously tenanted and arbitrarily named.

Having defined their origin, so far as we were able to do in the great obscurity of tradition and in the absence of contemporary evidence, we traced the variety of the discipline to which the several nations had been exposed between the dates of Clovis and Charles the Great. We saw Bavaria the creation of the Ostrogothic power, the close ally of Lombardy, the unwilling subject ally of the Austrasian kings, proud and uneasy under the yoke because it possessed a national character, a national history, and a national Christianity, which it did not owe to the Merovingian conquerors. Alemannia we saw lying quietly under the sway of the Frank kings, not possessing any territorial or dynastic unity, and, after the overthrow of the Burgundian kingdom, peacefully assimilating itself with the rest of the Frank empire.

Franconia and what was afterwards Lotharingia we regarded as integral and substantive portions of the demesne of the house of Clovis. Saxony continued heathen and hostile, and, forced by the constant pressure of the Wends on one side and the Franks on the other, into a national unity and consolidation, so marked and so lasting as to be one of the great features of German history, but of which we are unable to say how far it was created from a mass of tribal individualities by this pressure, or how far it retained the original unity of nationality which had subsisted from earlier times, and which, from the peculiarly free and popular character of the Saxon institutions, rendered it less likely to be broken up by the greed and ambition of individual leaders. Out of these distinct elements Charles the Great formed the medieval Germany; moving from the basis of Austrasia he reduced Bavaria, bereft of her mainstay on the Italian side in the Lombard kingdom, and he conquered the Saxons. He did more; by carrying his conquests beyond Bavaria and beyond Saxony he united the interests of the Saxons and Bavarians with those of his own house, with his own empire, and the interests of his own church. Charles the Great made Germany first by reducing it, and, secondly, by administering it.

The conversion of Saxony to Christianity supplied what was for a long time—that is, until the conversion of the Wends and Slavs—a more binding link between his German subjects than their own common origin and their own common tongue. But a stronger and a longer and a more equable pressure than any that Charles could bring to bear on the nations was necessary to keep Germany in the unity which he had for the moment produced. The divisions of the kingdoms under his sons, grandsons, and great-grandsons—divisions sometimes vertical and sometimes horizontal, but determined in detail rather by the ancient nationalities than by their more modern substitutes—tended rather perhaps to a laxity of friction than to any permanent disruption, but preserved and intensified the old lines of disunion. We do not indeed read again of the old Frank divisions of Neustria and Austrasia, nor even, in the same sense, of Aquitaine and Burgundy; but we have kings of Saxony, Franconia, Alemannia, and Bavaria, and the new name of Lotharingia, with its many differences of meaning and modifications of application.

Growth of Nationality.—And now we begin to trace in the nations distinct marks of policy and sentiment that long outlived the sentiment of nationality. We see in Franconia, the most anciently consolidated and completely feudalised of the nations, an exemplification of the identical causes which were producing disruption in Western France. Full of an ancient nobility rivals and enemies to one another ; smaller in territorial extent, and fuller of imperial cities than the other divisions, Franconia as a nation never exercises that influence on the German kingdom that Saxony and Bavaria do, and it is the first to disappear from the list of the great duchies of the imperial administration. Alemannia retains its character as an artificial construction such as it was when it originated in the congeries of broken Suevian tribes. Its territory, broken and rugged, divided, moreover, into two plain countries, Alsace and Swabia, separated by the forests, lakes, and mountains, rendered it especially liable to internal weakness : it is only after Swabia has permanently disengaged itself from Alsace and the intervening lands that it has such a unity as makes it under the Hohenstaufen and Welfs a real influence in Germany. Lotharingia, again, lies too much on one side of the kingdom to have a fair chance of deciding any contest, nor does Lotharingia once give a king to Germany so long as the strength of the German kingdom lasts. When the true life and spirit is departed we shall find her borrowing her rulers from Lotharingia in the house of Luxemburg whose reigns cover 150 of her weakest and most futile years. Saxony and Bavaria remain as the two great influences of German life in these ages. Saxony has been described as the most thorough and longest lived nationality, the last conquered and the least feudalised; possessing a greater number of ancient allodial Saxon nobles strong in the clannish affection of their followers; and in its comparatively free institutions a more permanent security for union than the casualties of conquest or the artificial uniting force of administration; and as it possessed the strongest national unity, we see it representing more strongly than the other nations the sentiment of German nationality.

Saxony.—Saxony is not only more thoroughly Saxon than Bavaria is Bavarian, but it is more thoroughly German than any of the other nations. This may be in a measure accounted for by the fact that Saxony was the first of the nations that acquired a hold on the royal dignity after the extinction of the Karlings, and that under Henry the Fowler and the three Ottos, Saxon princes, Germany awoke to the possibility of a working unity and to the possession of the empire. But it must have originated in something earlier and deeper, and that earlier and deeper sentiment can be attributed to nothing more certainly than to the comparative freedom of Saxony from Roman influence, her long and continued liberty, and the bracing character of her national institutions. And that it was not easily satisfied appears by the uneasiness of the nation even under Otto the Great after his imperial prospects in Italy had distracted and diverted his energies from their proper German work.

To go over this again would, however, be to run too much into detail, but I must add that the Saxon or German policy of the Saxons, which was to keep a Saxon on the throne, and, having him there, to keep him in Germany if not in Saxony itself—a strong

Saxon feeling that is tempered by the pride of having been the first of the nations to give a dynasty to Germany—is a clue to the position taken up by the Saxons generally with regard to the papacy. They were, it is true, probably better Christianised than the South Germans, though their Christianity was of later date and partook more strongly, as did that of Boniface their apostle, of devotion to the apostolic see. Their natural foes were the great prelates on the Rhine, whose constantly increasing power and ambition were met by a close alliance between the Saxons and Rome, whose rivals these prelates were. But there was still, I think, the powerful national instinct working with and giving energy to these accidental sentiments, that the German king was for Germany and not for Italy. The imperial idea met with very little support in this the least imperialised part of Germany.

Bavaria.—Contrasted with this is the position of South Germany, represented earlier by Bavaria and later by the Swabian princes. Bavaria, accustomed from the beginning to look towards Italy as in later times she has always looked towards France;[1] retaining throughout a pride of nationality, but not so much desiring, like Saxony, to give rulers to Germany, as to preserve her own identity as a national kingdom. Disabled by the extinction of her old royal house from creating a dynastic opposition to the imperial governors, but curiously assimilating those imperial governors to herself and making them, in spite of their own antecedents, the exponents of her national ambition, Bavaria, the representative nation of South Germany, clings most closely and faithfully to the shadow of the imperial dignity. We have seen exemplified under the Ottos

[1] *i.e.* till 1870.

this disintegrating tendency of Bavaria. A Saxon prince is made Duke of Bavaria; the Saxon becomes a Bavarian, and heads the opposition to his brother, nephew, and cousin. The Saxon dynasty ends, and a Bavarian duke ascends the throne, and resumes his Saxon character: but immediately Bavaria is in arms against him as king whom she has obeyed implicitly as duke; and so on, until the Welfic times into which new influences are imported and in which new features appear.

All this has been traced in its causes, and in some degree in its consequences, through the reigns of the Ottos and Henry II. Its consequences not less important but more remotely ran on even to 1870, the principle of national union being sought in North Germany the ancient Saxony, and that of disintegration being exemplified in Bavaria and in the foreign longings of Austria.

Growth of Feudalism.—But there are other influences besides nationality and the differences of national discipline which help to make up the history of the Middle Ages. There is the diffusion of feudalism, and there is the evoking and results of the counter influences of the empire and the papacy. The progress of feudalism, its gradual development, and the main distinctions between its effects in Germany and its effects in France, England, and Italy have already been exemplified. Nor is it indeed necessary to recapitulate them, for the distinctions originate chiefly on the growth of the institution and on the extent of the ground it gradually covers; once full grown and spread generally over a surface, its effects are much the same in all countries.

Feudal government, as distinguished from mere feudal tenure, grew up more slowly in Germany than in France, and was less universally diffused; but when it had come to its growth, and reached the extent of its diffusion, its tendency and effect was the same, to disruption, and the permanent division of the kingdom amongst a number of little potentates under nominal obedience to a suzerain. That nominal obedience in France had reality enough to be made under a series of strong and unscrupulous princes a basis of union.

French and German History compared.—From the twelfth century to the sixteenth the struggle between the princes and the crown continued, and at last France became one, at the price of becoming a kingdom absolutely governed. For in France the King of France was nothing but King of France; he had no other right to the obedience of his vassals, and only with the strong hand could he be content to govern them, or they to be governed. In Germany it was otherwise. Not only was the feudal principle less generally diffused and later in growth—that is, there were other tendencies towards disruption, as I have just shown, besides feudalism—but owing to circumstances even that modicum of uniting and centralising force which generally existed in feudalism at certain periods of its development was wanting in Germany; the principle of imperialism being substituted for it. The princes might be feudally subject to the emperor, or allodially free as the birds of the air, so far as their tenure was concerned, but as emperor they were all his subjects; and the force of the obligation to obedience being in the imperial dignity, not in the feudal relation only or primarily, the strength of the union varied directly with the reality or the unsubstantiality of the imperial power. And when the imperial power was distracted and diverted to Italy, as it was from the tenth century to the thirteenth, Germany lost the one force of cohesion she possessed; for feudalism could not support the strain for which in Germany it was not constituted, imperialism having taken its place.

And this accounts for the later differences between French and German history. The shadow, the dry bones of feudalism in France are revived and made the basis of a union under an absolute prince. Feudalism has no such uniting power in Germany. The imperial power becomes a nonentity, the imperial rights are bartered away for money, Germany ceases to have even a possibility of union. And happily, as she loses the possibility of union, she is saved from the payment of the price that France has paid. She remains disunited, but she continues free ; her institutions are deeply rooted in freedom : her little tyrants, where she has them, live on the affectionate sentiment that has survived the princes who deserved it, but at her worst estate she is not enslaved. France has become united, but as one nation of serfs.

Christianity in Germany.—It is necessary to mention the inferences to which our tracing of the early characteristics of feudal government have been leading us. One subject remains to be noticed before we bring down the result of our speculation to the point of actual history at which we are to begin. I mean the relations of Germany with the papacy, either through or independently of the imperial connection with it and Italy. First, then, of the condition of Christianity in Germany irrespective of the imperial complications.

Indirectly I have said a good deal about this in the former volume. We saw that the several nations had a distinct religious history as well as a distinct secular one. We accounted for the fact in the first place that Germany was untinged with Arianism, by showing that the Goths, who under Ulfilas had received the faith under that corrupt and heretical form with the other German tribes who were leavened from them, the Suevi and the Vandals, passed out of Germany long before the whole hive had heard the Gospel, and passed away southwards, to Italy, South France, Spain, and Africa, leaving not a single really German tribe in Germany affected by their heresy. That accounted for, we traced the Christianity of the Rhinelands to the Gallo-Roman times, and marked how largely they shared the secular features of Gallo-Roman Christianity in the unspiritual character of the clergy and the constant accumulation on the churches of secular privileges.

With the exception of the Rhinelands, all Germany owes its conversion to the awakened missionary energy of the sixth and seventh centuries. Bavaria, perhaps, first heard of Christianity from the Romans, but the religious work was completed by Celtic missionaries. Swabia, in like manner, received its apostles from the Scottish Churches. Franconia, partly from the Christianised energies of Clovis and the Gallo-Roman Church, partly from St. Kilian and other British or Scottish preachers sent out from the schools of Columbanus and Columba. Friesland—that is, the modern Holland and the country lying between it and Lower Saxony—was converted by Englishmen from Northumbria; Saxony, by Englishmen from Wessex. Of the several nations, Saxony only became a part of the Frank empire before it was Christianised; and not only did Saxony receive Christianity from the successors of Boniface in the field of missions, under the influence of Charles the Great, but the whole German Church was subjected to a like impulse under the same auspices, and raised from the low and secularised state into which religion under the Merovingian princes had fallen. This reformation and consolidation of the German Church under the influence, living and posthumous, of St. Boniface, had great effects. For the attitude of revived religion towards the papal see was different from that of the Franco-Gallican Church. Every reformation in learning, manners, morals, and discipline drew the Churches nearer to the centre of Apostolic teaching, and kindled the zeal of the defenders of Christianity in favour of the pope. The revival and spread of Christianity in France and Germany led almost directly to the formation of close relations between Pepin and Charles the Great on the one side, and Popes Zacharias, Stephen, Adrian, and Leo on the other. Charles Martel had died in deadly feud with the pope; Pepin laid the foundation of the temporal power; Charles destroyed the Lombards, and founded the Holy Empire. Still more was the German kingdom drawn to the papacy when the extension of the Gospel and the organisation of the Church in Saxony and beyond the true German lands among the Sclavonic tribes of the eastern marks had spread the influence of both pope and Cæsar.

During the century of the Karlings we lose sight in great measure of any peculiar characteristics of Teutonic Christianity; only we know that out of the obscurity emerge the False Decretals and the theories that have given shape to the modern domination of the Church of Rome. These were doubtless German in origin, for neither in the Gallican Church proper, nor in Italy, nor, least of all, in Rome itself, was there any disposition to recognise the supremacy in ecclesiastical discipline of the chair of St. Peter.

Relations with the Papacy.—We have come down to the time when it is impossible almost to distinguish between the German and the imperial relations with the papacy. And this was the second point. Henceforth in our study of German history we have to keep our eyes open, not only to the internal affairs of the kingdom, but to the perpetual seesaw between the Church and the empire. Pepin and Charles restore the strength of the papacy, or, perhaps, we might say, create it; in return the popes create Pepin king of the Franks, Charles emperor of the Romans. The Karling century sees the popes gradually sinking in moral status, and German influence being paralysed by the contentions of the family, under Italian influence of the worst and pettiest kind, Italianising and demoralising the Church. Out of this moral abyss the papacy was rescued by Otto, as it had been out of the political one by Pepin and Charles, and again the reward was the imperial crown. The regenerating influence of Germany on Rome lasted for nearly a century of action and reaction. The idea of righteousness culminated in Otto III.; the practical summit was attained by Henry III.:—from the death of Henry the two influences change places: that of the papacy becomes righteous, pure, and ideal, that of the empire becomes despotic, immoral, material. Unhappily the revived consciousness of the papacy sees its only policy in the humiliation of the empire, and, by good and evil, by doing much and suffering more, it did succeed; and in the humiliation of Henry IV. it found a set-off to the many energetic castigations that it had received from German hands. But as the revived spirituality of Rome, represented by such men as Gregory VII., Urban II., and Paschal II., Anselm of Canterbury, and Bernard of Clairvaux, did gradually evaporate during the twelfth century, it left the struggle devoid of its old moral and religious interest, and substantially political, political only. The ideal sought is not now righteousness or reformation, but simply power. It is not the vindication or reduction of ecclesiastical freedom, but merely the attaining of an independent influence in the balance of the European powers. The popes wish to expel the empire from Italy; the emperor wishes to retain his hold upon it, and that by his hold on the pope.

We no longer have contrasts between a virtuous emperor and an immoral pope, or between an ascetic pope and a profligate emperor: the popes are neither above nor below the ecclesiastical morality of the age reformed by St. Bernard; the emperors, although, as usual, intellectually and morally superior to the common run of princes, do not find that either knowledge or virtue gives them any advantage in the political strife.

Imperial Policy.—But putting aside ideas for facts, we have traced the alteration of relations between Henry IV. and Gregory VII. for a century after the death of both. We have marked how the lines of party in Germany, the Welfs and Waibelings, or Guelfs and Ghibellines, are drawn upon ancient divisions, although the parties themselves are inspired with new sentiments in addition to their old rivalries. Of course, North Germany, intensely German and religious, anti-imperial, and by consequence papal, governed by rulers who owe the affections of their subjects rather to their ancient national importance than to the loyalty felt towards imperial functionaries, is matched against South Germany, the home of the Hohenstaufens, the constant treasurer of imperial traditions. Saxony, the constant ally under all her different dynasties of the papal see, is exposed more especially also to the aggressions of those spiritual princes of the Rhine whose policy has been imperial as opposed to papal, because imperialism meant to them secular independence, and papalism meant practical insignificance. These princes, constantly buying, borrowing, or stealing secular privileges from the empire, and again purchasing confirmations and immunities from Rome, win a large stake at each turn of the game. They find it a source of strength to be without that which is the source of strength to the temporal princes, hereditary succession. The emperor whose influence is generally enough to secure the election of his nominee is not afraid that he will create a new competitor for empire or found a rival dynasty. Dukes and counts, margraves and landgraves have done so; it is only on rare chances of escheat that the appointment to these functions falls into the emperor's hands, and when it does he is restricted by the force of political opinion from making a selfish use of his chances, whilst the appointments, once made, proceed on the principle of hereditary succession, with which he can interfere only at deadly peril to himself and his family. There is no fear of this in the clerical principalities. He can make an old tutor, or a bastard brother, an archbishop, and as archbishop load him with secular power, without fear of finding him a traitor or the founder of a new rival race. So the old duchies, and especially Saxony, have their jurisdictions limited and their very territories dismembered in favour of a hierarchy which may be trusted to be faithfully imperial. Hence the spiritual princes have the enormous influence in North Germany which colours the whole later medieval history; hence their great weight in the election of the emperor; hence their opposition to the national instinct of North Germany, their share in the revulsion of feeling in those lands with regard to the papacy which facilitated the reformation in the sixteenth century.

But in this part of the imperial policy there was one weak point, and that the popes knew how to take advantage of. The spiritual princes, much as they loved the empire and the emperor, loved themselves more, and could not shut their eyes to the fact that they were spiritual princes over a people amenable in an especial degree to spiritual menaces. Hence the wonderful power of excommunication in the hands of the popes against the emperors; hence the moral necessity in the emperors' eyes for an antipope; and from that necessity the equally pressing one of retaining some hold on the right of influencing papal elections. Independently of a mere Italian policy, the emperor must be able to protect his spiritual princes against the consequences of papal excommunication: that he can do only by the creation of a rival pope; but the world will not recognise his rights to nominate an antipope unless he is able to prove and also to vindicate his right to appoint the regular pope in a vacancy.

The difference between the effects of interdicts and excommunication in Germany, and its effects in France and England, are very marked. In England it was indeed only tried in the reign of John, and then only a few of the bishops recognised it, whilst it had no influence for the time on the politics of the kingdom. In France, king after king defied the weapon without the loss apparently of political strength. But in Germany, nominally and deeply divided, only needing a shock to produce disruption, leavened so largely and widely with politico-spiritual influences, the bolt was fatal at once. It not only released the unfaithful from the necessity of feigning obedience, but it disarmed and paralysed those who would have been most faithful. Witness the history of Henry IV., Henry V., Otto IV., and Frederick II.

Frederick Barbarossa.—Frederick Barbarossa, alone at the head of a singularly united Germany, and acting in co-operation with antipopes above the usual type, is able to maintain an equal fight with the pope even in exile. And the humiliation of Frederick Barbarossa after the battle of Legnano, and in the peace of Venice, although it is less picturesque, and indeed less morally touching than that of his predecessors and successors, is not less a political defeat of enormous importance; important both because of the majesty and nobility of the hero who maintains his character and loses not an iota of respect where he is obliged to yield the fruits of a life's struggle; and also because of the singular weakness and disjointedness of the league before which he succumbs, between an exile of popes, an upstart Norman king, and a few outlawed and often plundered Italian towns. Germany was indeed united under him, but the pope made for him a foe in his own household. Henry the Lion, the Welf, the Saxon hero, the friend of Becket, the conqueror and Christianiser of the Slavs, would no longer fight against the pope, when he saw his cousin's chief minister, Philip of Heinsberg, Archbishop of Cologne, the foe to the pope, but much more the foe to himself, a rival aiming at and content with nothing less than the dismemberment of Saxony.

Germany in the Thirteenth Century.—So all these forces play into one another's directions, and the resultant is what we are now come to. The reign of Frederick II. broke up the empire, and broke up what was not at all in the nature of things bound up with the empire, the unity of Germany. I need not recapitulate a recapitulation. It was the fatal union with Italy that precipitated the result: the fatal union with Rome first, and the finally fatal union with

B

Sicily. Italy itself was enough to paralyse any ordinary prince's energy; but Italy with Sicily and Jerusalem was too much for the grand genius, power, intellect, and protracted reign of Frederick II. Where the imperial energies were spent outside of Germany, no wonder that Germany went its own way. But this had been so before, under both weak kings and strong, and yet the mass had been brought again together. Under the most brilliant of the Cæsars the ruin came, and without remedy. Much, of course, was owing to the very brilliancy and eccentric power of Frederick, to the hatreds he inspired, and the recklessness with which he inspired men with them. Something in Italy was due no doubt to the ability and persistent policy of his enemies the popes. But in Germany nothing or very little can be attributed to these things.

In Germany the catastrophe depended far more on political than on personal causes. It is curious how little of his reign was spent in Germany itself: he must have been known far more by report than in person; and perhaps it may have been that his fall was occasioned rather by his absence from the country than by his unpopularity in it. But after all, although the occasion was this, the causes were far older and more effective. Germany began the reign of Frederick apparently the Germany of old; she came out of it a body with new names, and new powers, and functions. This is seen in the gradual break-up of the old duchies. The early division of Franconia and extinction of the Franconian line in the person of Henry V.; the dismemberment of Saxony and Bavaria under the forfeiture of Henry the Lion, and the creation of new and insignificant dukedoms out of his magnificent inheritances; the virtual dismemberment of Swabia by the extravagance and short-sighted policy of Philip, King of Germany, who raised funds for his resistance to Otto IV., by the sale of the imperial rights over towns and vassals ; the making of all these small powers which arose from the dismemberment of the greater ones, immediately subject to the empire, so that by sale or gift they were able constantly to wring from the emperor privileges which made them really sovereign each in his own little territory ; the impoverishment of the imperial domain going on coincidently with the loss of feudal rights and revenues from the lands not in demesne—all this was reducing the emperor to the condition of an honorary or titular prince, who but for the prestige of his title, and the hereditary dominions which as count or duke he might have had before he attained the imperial title, had little more real power in his dominions than the titular kings of Achaia and Jerusalem, or the later Roman emperors.

So much then, for the present, of the principles, the broad lines of politics, the elements of political life, the causes and consequences which we have seen hitherto at work in German history. We have henceforth to contemplate it under new conditions springing directly out of the old, but differing in form and favour. I shall begin with a short view of the actual events of German history under Frederick II., Conrad, and Conradin ; but the most important portion of this volume will begin with the interregnum, and be devoted to the far more prosaic and humdrum course of events, politics, and development of institutions which we shall have to trace under the princes of Hapsburg, Bavaria, and Luxemburg. We pass from the golden at once to the copper, and brass, and iron age : we lose our last glimpse of the heroes with Frederick Barbarossa, the old knight-errant, riding away into the land of paynim giants and monsters, or appearing, to their mutual wonder, to the lost shepherd among the caves of the Harz and Salzburg mountains, never, alas! to return.

IMPORTANT DATES

Death of Frederick Barbarossa, 1190.
Reign of Henry VI., 1190–1197.
Philip, 1198–1208.
Otto IV., 1198–1215.
Frederick II., 1212–1250.

*

*

CHAPTER II

The Reign of Frederick II.—It may be regarded as one of the commonplaces of history, to represent the reign of Frederick II. as a very epitome and concentration of all that has gone before that is interesting and significant in the life of the empire. Not only does the character of the emperor seem to embrace all the salient characteristics of his predecessors, but the very events are a reiteration, and the very combinations a repetition of the mixture of ingredients of former periods of development. In Frederick we see not only the brilliant ability and high ideal of Otto III., but the strength in action of Henry III., and the spirit, brave, adventurous, and impetuous, of Frederick Barbarossa; but also we see, not less clearly, all the profligacy of Henry IV., and the unprincipled cruelty of Otto II. and Henry VI. As the chosen defender of the papacy, he recalls to our minds the original conditions of the empire, the delivering hand of Pepin and Charles and Otto, armed with the same strength, and purchasing advancement by the same gifts of lands and power bestowed in fact or in promise on the papacy. In his later assumption of independence as against papal interference and supremacy, we see the same revulsion of feeling that we saw in Henry V., who having as defender of the Church dethroned his father, as his father's successor bent all his energies to the humiliation of the Church. In his antagonism with the popes, the struggle with his own son, whom the Italian alliance had set against him, in his humiliation and final fall, we read again, although with many differences of circumstances, the story of Henry IV.

But no accumulation of such details should divert us from seeing, that in reality all that is touching and dramatic in the biography of Frederick belongs to Italy and not to Germany. The origin of all his greatness, his brilliant successes, and his great humiliations, was not in Germany. His birth and education, his temper, his faults and his merits, were Italian. Henry VI. had laid the foundation of his miseries in the Sicilian marriage, and in the means he took to secure to his son the inheritance of the whole of his own and his wife's dominions. The Sicilian kingdom, the guerdon as the popes chose to regard it, or wages of the servants and defenders of Rome, was to be, according to Henry VI.'s plan, united for ever to the imperial dignity, and that dignity to become hereditary. This the popes might well object to ; they lost the cherished obedience of the Sicilian kings, and saw their pet fief go to strengthen the hands of their would-be masters. The childhood of Frederick was the great opportunity for the popes. A Welf emperor was elected under papal influence to break at once the continuity of Henry VI.'s policy : when that Welf emperor found to his cost that the attitude of rivalry with the pope was inseparable from the status of emperor, whether Welf or Waibeling, danger from the young heir of Hohenstaufen seemed to the pope to be so remote that he himself brought him forward as the

rival of the unfortunate Otto. Nor was it until Frederick
had, by eight years spent in Germany, and by the death
of Otto and collapse of the Welfic interest in North Germany, consolidated his power in a way that recalled the
popes to their old policy that the struggle again broke
out. The struggle beginning with the point at which it
had been left by Henry VI., the union of the crowns of
the empire and of Sicily on one head. This was the *fons
et origo mali;* other grudges and hatreds entered largely
into the struggle, until it became one of personal persecution and extermination. But the scene of the wars,
the interest of the adventures lies in Italy, Sicily, and
Palestine, and the indirect effects of these upon Germany
it is not difficult to sum up; they have, in fact, been
summed up briefly in the previous volume.[1]

His Love of Italy.—The reign of Frederick extends
from 1212 to 1250; from his first attempt to assert
a right to the empire, an attempt wonderfully successful and brilliant, to his death. In 1218 he was
relieved from the rivalry, long ago practically extinct,
of Otto, and two years after he obtained the imperial
crown: that imperial crown he wore, if we accept
his deposition by Innocent IV., until 1245, or twenty-
five years; if we ignore that, for thirty years, ending
with his death in 1250. Of the thirty-eight years
which include his whole connection with Germany he
spent not more than twelve on this side of the Alps:
from 1212 to 1220 he was in Germany; only two years,
July 1235 to August 1237, of his imperial reign were
spent there. He was, notwithstanding, regarded with
honour and affection, won probably by his early graces,
and by the inherited title to reverence earned by the
house of Hohenstaufen. We have had occasion to

[1] " Germany in the Early Middle Ages."

remark before how strong the hereditary instinct was in
Germany, although it was not legally the theory of the
kingdom or empire. The third generation of a dynasty
had outlived all competition, in the cases of Otto III.,
Henry V., and Henry VI. No duke or prince was a
likely rival to the heir of Hohenstaufen when he was
once come to man's estate. With the assumption of the
imperial crown, Frederick's close intercourse with Germany ended. Again the fatal gift of Italian supremacy
destroys the health of Germany. Frederick, in 1220, left
his kingdom north of the Alps, and only once returned
to it, after a lapse of fifteen years. For these fifteen
years his eldest son Henry, eight years old at the time of
his election as King of the Romans, acted as his father's
representative. He was elected at Frankfort in 1220,
without the consent of the pope, and in defiance of the
papal policy; but the pope, who was ready for the time
to sacrifice everything for the prospect of the Crusade,
accepted Frederick's assertion that he did not intend to
unite permanently Naples and Sicily with the empire,
but only wished to provide for the proper government
of his states whilst he was absent on the Crusade, and
crowned him emperor in the winter of the same year.

The eight years from 1212 to 1220 were, after the
struggle with Otto IV. had subsided, years of comparative security. Frederick was very popular; he found
means of attaching the princes to himself; the extinction
of the dukes of Zahringen, and the humiliation of the
Welfs, gave him the means of rewarding faithful service,
and the support of the prelates he purchased with the
grant of very extensive privileges. Amongst others, he
surrendered the right of seizing on the personal effects
of prelates at their death, and the right of coining money
and exacting toll within their territories; he protected

their churches against the oppressions of their official
advocates or defenders, and he enforced the authority
of sentences of the Church by placing contemners
under the bann of the empire.[1] It was by these that
he won the consent of the clerical members of the diet
to the election of his son as King of the Romans.

His son Henry.—Well, Frederick being out of sight,
gone to Italy for fifteen years, the young Henry becomes
the centre of German interest. For five years, 1220 to
1225, he was under the tutelage of Archbishop Engelbert
of Cologne, to whom is commonly ascribed the introduction of the *Vehmgericht* in Westphalia, and who, by
his inflexible administration, at once ensured the security
of the kingdom and brought about his own death; for in
1225 he was assassinated by the Count of Isenberg, whom
he had offended by his rigour. Henry was crowned, by
Engelbert, king as Henry VII., at Aix-la-Chapelle in
1222. In 1223 he compelled the King of Denmark to
receive his crown as a vassal. On Engelbert's death the
emperor appointed as guardian of his son, and vicar of
the empire, Lewis, Duke of Bavaria and Count Palatine
of the Rhine—a Wittelsbach by race and a representative
of the new order of things resulting from the breaking
up of the old duchies. He was the son of that Otto who
had succeeded to Bavaria on the forfeiture of Henry
the Lion in 1180, and he had himself succeeded to the
County Palatine partly as son-in-law and partly as
substitute for Henry of Saxony the son of Henry the
Lion. He represented, then, in a way, both Welf and
Waibeling interests, and was destined to lead his ward
into difficulties that ended in his destruction. The house
which he founded in Bavaria and in the Palatinate was
the one which more than any other throughout the

---

[1] Milman, "History of Latin Christianity," vol. v. p. 62.

later Middle Ages keeps up the idea of the old position of the duchies : in it Bavaria made several bold and partly successful bids for empire, and it is the only one of the German houses which now exist, except the Welfs themselves, that has maintained itself in the male line to the present day. Lewis of Wittelsbach occupied the important place in which Frederick's confidence had put him for six years, when in 1231 he also was assassinated.

The Relations of Frederick with Henry.—It may be that subsequent events have cast a false reflection over the acts of Frederick at this period. But, true or false, it was believed that the emperor suspected Lewis of an attempt to withdraw Henry from allegiance to his father, and that the assassin, an unknown person, was an Egyptian sent from Syria for the purpose, by the Old Man of the Mountain, with whom Frederick in his crusade had entered into an alliance. Frederick at this time had just made his peace with the pope, and was looking about him no doubt with a view to making security doubly secure. But the motive, and indeed the deed itself, is a mystery.

The next nine years were peaceful years for Italy. Frederick continued on good terms, or on quiet terms at least, until 1239, and betook himself to legislation and the cultivation of arts, science, and wickedness in his favourite kingdom. His great trouble during these years was from Germany; and even this storm blew from the Italian side of the Alps. Henry, in 1227, had married Margaret, daughter of the Duke of Austria, and after the murder of Lewis of Wittelsbach seems to have got on tolerably well for two or three years without a guardian ; he was, indeed, now twenty years old. There can be little doubt that the contemporary writers were justified in their suspicions that Henry had been tampered with by the pope during his father's extraordinary crusade—that in which, you will remember, the emperor, whilst under the sentence of excommunication, recovered the Holy City. Either Henry was at that time alienated from his father by the same unholy policy that had set Conrad in opposition to Henry IV., or suspicions were insinuated into the mind of Frederick that it was so, which suspicions worked out their own confirmation. I do not know that it implies a more than usual baseness in Henry that he formed designs against the father whom he had seen but once (at Aquileia in 1232) since he was eight years old, and of whom all he heard was his impiety and his lavish affection for his other children.

Conrad, the son of Yolanda of Jerusalem, and the unhappy successor of both father and brother, seems to have been placed before young Henry as his especial rival, and he was told that he was to supplant him in the succession. Neither in Germany nor in Italy were wanting influences available in favour of the papal and opposed to the imperial plan, and as early as 1231 he had endeavoured, by an enactment in favour of the princes, placing the local jurisdiction in their hands instead of those of the imperial officers, to make himself a party against Frederick; but Frederick disarmed the conspirators by confirming the edict, and pardoned his penitent son at Aquileia. With these Henry was persuaded to take counsel. But in 1234 the Milanese, by ambassadors, opened negotiations with him, and in a meeting of the princes, a conspiracy was formed to help him in the ambition of becoming independent of his father. It does not appear that the conspiracy was a very strong one, or that it proceeded to much overt action. Frederick was too prompt for it, and he wisely trusted to his own popularity. He hastened into Germany in the spring of 1235, and early in July, at Worms, received his son into his favour.

Hermann of Salza, the Grand Master of the Teutonic Knights, and Frederick's wisest and most faithful counsellor, acted as mediator. Henry pretended to submit, but almost immediately after the reconciliation provoked his father again by refusing to surrender the castle of Trifels and to perform other conditions. He was accordingly arrested within a few days of the pardon, and committed to the charge of Otto, the Count Palatine, at Heidelberg; thence he was removed to Alzen, and thence to Sicily, where he lingered in chains until February 1242, when he died at Martorano in Apulia and was buried at Cosenza.

" *Frederick's Wives.*—The conduct of both father and son is matter of considerable obscurity. We are at a loss to estimate the character of the provocation which met with so severe a punishment: so savage a one indeed, if we may believe the enemies of Frederick in their assertion that he starved his son to death. The history of Henry is, on the other hand, misrepresented by the advocates of Frederick in a way that is outrageously unhistorical.[1] Facts speak for themselves, and I cannot think that the right was altogether on the side of the father who, notwithstanding the passionate lamentation over his son which he penned on the occasion, within a fortnight of the condemnation of his son to perpetual imprisonment, celebrated his third marriage with great pomp and luxury in the very town, Worms, where the unhappy Henry was a captive. Frederick's third wife was Isabella of England, daughter

---

[1] *Menzel is especially inaccurate.*

of John, sister of Henry III. and of Richard of Cornwall, afterwards King of the Romans; his second was Queen Yolanda of Jerusalem; his first had been Constance of Castile, also a granddaughter of our King Henry II.

The Diet at Mainz.—A week after the wedding Frederick held a great diet at Mainz, at which the deposition of Henry was formally transacted, and an ordinance put out by the emperor, in the German language, relating to the general condition and constitution of the kingdom. It seems to have been intended as a remedial act, to protect the imperial power from the losses which had been inflicted by the rash measures of Henry, and which Frederick, in self-defence or policy, had for the moment confirmed. But the time was past when it was possible to reduce Germany under a regular imperial organisation; and Frederick probably saw that this was the case. Another and a better policy was to endeavour to strengthen the influence of law and of the imperial authority, by confirming and increasing the privileges of the imperial cities. No doubt he had found by experience of Italy the strength and permanence of the civic institution, and was willing to take pains to secure on his own side in Germany an element of society so stable and whose interests were bound up so closely with the maintenance of law, and resistance of feudal oppression at the hand of their common foes. I dare not say that this actually was so: I am not sure that Frederick really cared about Germany any further than touched his own interest: he could not have loved it and be content to see so little of it; and it may have been that, like our own kings, he sold privileges and charters merely to raise money.

Another act of some historical significance that marks

this diet, is the erection of Lüneburg and Brunswick into a duchy in favour of Otto the Child, son of William of Winchester and grandson of Henry the Lion. It marks the extinction of the part of the Welfic house of their old claims to a rivalry with the imperial house; the family that had once ruled from the Baltic to the Tiber is now content with a newly created and comparatively small duchy. But they had undergone great humiliations since the time of Otto IV.; still retaining these ancient allods of their Saxon forefathers, although the tenure was changed into that of a fief by surrender and reinvestiture, they possessed a basis on which future power could be and actually was raised.

Frederick in Germany.—Frederick's visit to Germany lasted two years: during this time, after the immediate pressure of public business was over, he travelled through the country endeavouring to inspire regard by his popular manners, and awe by the oriental magnificence of his court: everywhere granting and confirming liberties, and, notwithstanding his Edict of Mainz, recognising the prescriptive infringements by the princes of the few remaining imperial prerogatives. Amongst other acts of the kind was his declaration of all his hereditary estates in Germany to be the property of the crown, and his raising his personal vassals to the station of tenants in chief of the empire; thus completing that break-up of the old subordination of the feudal empire which had been going on since the partition of the Welfic dominions. He had been recalled into Lombardy in the winter of 1236 by the war with the republics, but even this he was obliged to leave unfinished and to turn back into Austria for the humiliation of Frederick, the warlike Duke of Austria, whose turbulence and love of war kept the whole relations of Bohemia and the eastern parts of Germany in a turmoil. Frederick was condemned to forfeiture in a diet at Augsburg in 1236, after which he was obliged to be quiet for some years. The emperor himself spent some months at Vienna after this, and having traversed central Germany in 1237, returned to Italy in September.

The visits may be regarded as one, broken by the short Italian campaign. It was at Vienna that he made arrangements for the government of Germany in his absence. He had not learned wisdom from the rebellion of Henry, or else his affection for his second son overcame his prudence. Conrad, the son of Yolanda of Brienne, only eleven years old, was to be his substitute; the election was made at Vienna by the Archbishops of Mainz and Trèves, the Duke of Bavaria, who was also Count Palatine, and the King of Bohemia. It was confirmed at Spires by the assembled diet in July, and Frederick finally shook himself free of his German subjects. Briefly to sum up: the share taken by the Lombard cities in the perversion and rebellion of Henry provoked Frederick to determine on their destruction. All the rest of his history follows logically upon this quarrel.

Frederick and Gregory IX.—On his return from Germany he devoted himself entirely to this purpose, and for a time seemed likely to succeed. In November 1237 he won, at Corte Nuova, a complete and apparently decisive victory; and at last it seemed probable that the imperial dream would be fulfilled. But when matters appeared worst for Italy and the papacy, suddenly the tide turned, and the abuse of victory roused a resistance that was destined after many vicissitudes to be victorious. Gregory IX. determined to throw the whole power of the Church into the scale

against Frederick; and Frederick's sins and errors,
real or imputed, had been accumulating during many
years, only a few of which misdoings would have been
enough for a damnatory charge against him. His successes in 1238 were less decisive than they had been in
the former year; he was forced to retire from Brescia.
Then the pope concluded a league against him with
Venice and the remaining supports of Italian liberty.
Having prepared his material weapons, he opened the
war with a spiritual denunciation; in March 1239 he
excommunicated Frederick.

The time was hardly come for excommunication to
take immediate effect: a curious paper war followed;
both pope and emperor addressing long letters of appeal and defence to the princes of Europe. Frederick
had still a strong hold on the affections of Germany,
and there the effect of the papal fulmination, sure but
slow, was impeded by the attempt of the pope to urge
the election of an anti-Cæsar in the person of Robert of
France, the brother of St. Louis. St. Louis, on the
occasion, behaved in a way worthy of his great name;
he not only in the most dignified manner rebuked the
pope for his presumption and the unspiritual character of his policy, but communicated to Frederick the
machinations which were being laid against him. In
Germany itself the proposal strengthened for the
moment the hands of the emperor, and the arrogance
and misconduct of the papal legate, provoked to the
last degree the ecclesiastical princes whose faith was
most likely to be affected by the excommunication.
So long as Gregory lived Frederick pushed his successes
in Italy with hardly a drawback.

Frederick's Death, 1250.—The pope died in 1241, and
the election of a successor was delayed for two years.

At last Innocent IV., a personal adherent of Frederick, was elected, and after some troublesome negotiations peace was made between pope and emperor in March 1244. But within three months of the treaty Innocent fled secretly from Rome to France, and began the series of aggressions which ended in the fall of Frederick. In the Council of Lyons he not only renewed the excommunication, but declared the emperor deposed, and preached a crusade against him. From this moment every nerve that could be strained on the part of the papacy was strained, and although for two or three years Frederick's genius warded off the fatal end, his signal discomfiture before Parma in August 1247, which Milman calls the turning-point of his fortunes, seems to have broken his spirit or disturbed the balance of his mind. He struggled on for a couple of years more with energies paralysed and a heart broken by the misfortunes of his children and the reputed treachery of his friends. The captivity of his son Enzio, and the treason of Peter de Vinea, his prime minister, were too much for him. He became almost frantic, and yet irresolute and practically inactive. This period of his life closed only with it; he died at Fiorentino in December 1250, leaving to his children a small share of his genius, and the full inheritance of his sins and misfortunes.

The Importance of his Reign.—In this chapter, which is only intended as an introduction to the state of things which follow the death of Frederick, it is not necessary to go into minute particulars of dates, names, and places. But the historians of the time are themselves far from being liberal of such indications. In truth, Frederick's personal history occupies not indeed a greater share of the historian's attention

c

than it deserves, but more than is proportional to it in relation with the general history of the times. He had reigned so long, and his abilities, his power, and his adventures had made him so famous that the writers of the time looked on his history as the general history of the world. And their example has been followed by later historians with more excuse. The result of this is that there is much obscurity in every department that lies outside the sphere of his personal action. We are left in ignorance even as to who were the guardians and chief ministers of the little King Conrad during the earlier years of his lieutenancy in Germany. Dietrich, Archbishop of Trèves, was guardian in 1242. It is only discoverable by inference that Duke Otto of Bavaria discharged towards him the duties that his father Lewis had done for King Henry. Otto maintained the Hohenstaufen interest in Germany as long as it could be maintained; he refused to act upon the excommunication of 1239, and even when, two years later, the ecclesiastical princes changed sides, remained faithful to Frederick. The Duke of Austria, also Frederick the Warlike, returned to his allegiance after four years of forfeiture, and was restored by the emperor with increased and accumulated honours. Swabia was under the personal rule of the young Conrad, and there was thus no danger of the imperial cause being lost in South Germany.

The Tartars.—During these few years, during which the papal policy was working secretly rather than overtly in Germany, the great event to be noticed is the threat of a barbarian invasion on the side of Hungary. Genghis Khan had founded a great Tartar empire earlier in the century. Batou Khan, his grandson, as lieutenant of the great Mongol Emperor Octai, directed his conquering energies westward. Ravaging Russia and Poland, he

reached the borders of Germany. In 1241 he entered
Silesia. Slavs and Germans alike fled before him or
perished in unavailing resistance · turned aside by the
obstinacy of Breslau, and deterred by a storm which
excited his superstitious fears, he moved southward
towards Hungary. All Germany was summoned to the
rescue. Enzio was sent from Italy by the emperor to
assist Conrad, and under the command of Conrad the
army of Batou was met near the Danube and defeated.
Batou retired, but Hungary had almost perished under
the infliction. Bela, the king, having been driven into
Dalmatia, purchased the aid of Frederick for his restoration and for securing his dominions, it is said, by surrendering the feudal domination of Hungary to the
empire. This, like every question on the relations of
Hungary to Germany, is obscure. And it is not less an
illustration of the obscurity of the details of the time
that the place at which this decisive battle was fought,
one which, humanly speaking, saved Europe from being
conquered and reduced to barbarism, is unknown.
Milman calls the stream on which it was fought
Delphos ; but although Moravia and Austria itself
abounds with relics and traditions of the invasion, we
only know that the battle took place near the Danube
and sometime in the year 1241.

Germany, 1239-1254.—It has been said that the effects
of the papal excommunication of 1239 were slow but
sure. It is in 1241 that we first trace their operation
in Germany. At this time the ecclesiastical princes
were still faithful; and the papal diplomatists rested
their hopes rather on Bavaria and Austria than on
the bishops. A conference was held at Budweis in
September 1241 on the expediency of a new election.
But singularly the two great powers, the temporal

and spiritual, either changed sides or were obliged
to renounce their temporising policy and show their
true colours. Bavaria, Bohemia, and Austria, on whom
the papal party had relied, adhered to Frederick;
but the machinations of the legate produced a counter
move among the bishops. Frederick, learning that their
allegiance was questionable, widened the breach by his
violent and insulting language; and a league was formed
against him. The crown was offered by this party first
to Otto of Bavaria, and by him rejected with scorn.

The deposition of Frederick in 1245 strengthened the
party greatly; but no one would yet consent to be
anti-Cæsar. The King of Bohemia, the Dukes of Austria,
Brabant, and Saxony, and the Margraves of Meissen
and Brandenburg, refused it. At length an election was
made at Hochheim, near Wurzburg, on Ascension Day,
1246. The great majority of princes present were
ecclesiastical; the four archbishops, Mainz, Trèves,
Cologne, and Bremen, the Bishops of Metz, Spires, and
Strassburg; a very few insignificant lay princes joined in
the act. By the influence of the Archbishop of Cologne,
who throughout was a strong papal partisan, Henry,
surnamed Raspo, Landgrave of Thuringia, was elected.
He was crowned and placed at the head of a crusading
army mustered by the Archbishop of Mainz. War
began immediately. Henry, the priests' king (*Pfaffenkönig*), defeated King Conrad near Frankfort on August 5.
Conrad's Swabian soldiers deserted him, and Henry
seemed in a likely way to supplant his rival altogether;
but his success was not lasting; he was prevented by
the severity of the winter from carrying out the complete subjugation of Swabia, and having retired into his
hereditary states, died a natural death in February 1247.

In the autumn of the same year a new king of the

Romans was chosen, William, Count of Holland.   Before
his rising star the fortunes of Conrad waned rapidly.   In
1248 he was compelled to fly into Italy, where he shared
his father's few remaining misfortunes.   We lose sight of
him in Germany for two years.   He seems, however, to
have returned before his father's death, and to have
maintained some show of authority in Swabia and
Bavaria.   But gradually he was left friendless in Germany, and retreated into the safe kingdom of Apulia.
There, however, the unrelenting hostility of Innocent IV.
pursued him with excommunication.   His fortunes
seemed to be rising when he died in 1254, under strong
suspicion of being poisoned.

The End of the Hohenstaufens.—The romantic history
of Conradin does not belong to Germany.   The internal
events of these years will be described in the next
chapter in connection with William of Holland, Richard
of Cornwall, and the great Interregnum.   We will now
very briefly comment on the end of the old imperial
régime under the last of the Hohenstaufen.   It seems
curious, but I conceive it to be the truth, that the
possession of Italy was the fatal, vulnerable, incurable
point in the lot of Frederick II.   It was not so much
his absence from Germany, because that we saw after
many years had not impaired his popularity, and there
were many reasons why the absence of a supreme
check on ambitious princes should make the absentee
emperor more acceptable than a present one would
be.   There was absolutely no family left in Germany,
north or south, which could enter into a moment's
competition with him.   The faithfulness of Germany
was proved, moreover, by the length of time that
it survived the trying ordeal of the papal excommunication of the emperor.   During his earlier diffi-

culty with Gregory IX. about the Crusade, Germany never wavered: after the second excommunication it was two years before the election of a successor was mooted; and then the attempt was a failure. It was not until 1246—that is, seven years after the second excommunication—and not until six or seven of the lay princes had refused the empire, that Henry of Thuringia, under strict papal orders, as strict as those by which he appointed to a bishopric, ventured to accept the proffered honour. It is true that, once done, Frederick's fortunes went downhill very rapidly, but that they did in Italy, where his own presence failed to restore them, as well as in Germany. If Frederick would yet have shown himself north of the Alps, he might have still retrieved his fortunes. Italy and Sicily, as subsequent events showed, might have been confidently entrusted to his sons. For Italy he lost his last hold on Germany; he ,had willingly deserted her; he had alienated his natural friends, the prelates; he had neglected those who beyond all hopes had shown themselves his friends, the princes. He had parted with the legal rights of the crown, divested himself personally of his own hereditary states in Germany—and all for Italy.

Germany under Frederick II. — All the glory and brilliancy of Frederick is, to my mind, extinguished in the dereliction of his duty as a German sovereign. All his love was spent on the kingdoms of his mother, and the attempt to effect what Frederick Barbarossa had failed to effect—what the policy of the papal see, which in the long run was backed up by Christendom, would not endure to see—the absolute conquest of North Italy and the isolation of the Patrimony of St. Peter. The worshippers of the imperial ideal see nothing in Frederick that is not admirable: the

admirers of the papal ideal, on the contrary, regard him
as little else than Antichrist.   But why the Germans
should regard him as a sovereign to be admired or loved,
I see no reason, except in the inherited reverence of his
family, and perhaps a sort of pride that a German prince
should make such a figure in the world.   It is to Frederick II. and his father and uncle, Henry VI. and Philip
of Swabia, that Germany owes the fate that fell on her
in the thirteenth century, of being, in spite of her extent,
the wealth and intelligence of her people, the multitudes
of her noble warriors, and the eminence of individuals
amongst her sons in every description of human excel-
lence, as a whole, as a nation, a kingdom, an empire,
practically impotent in Europe for two centuries and
more; and, further, that when the time came for a
sufficiently large portion of her territory to be united
under two or three great families, so much of her energy
was employed upon internal struggles.

In the twelfth century there was still a chance that
the several nations who combined into the German
kingdom might combine into a German nation.   Great
as were the hindrances in variety of language, of tradition, of tribal institutions and character under Frederick
Barbarossa, they were less than they had ever been
before; the great duchies were being gradually broken
up into small jurisdictions, none of which might be
strong enough to defy the supreme power or enter
into rivalry with it.   The fragments were broken small,
to be, if the hand had been there to do it, forced into a
compact and equable mass.   But when the amalgamating
force was needed, Germany was left alone; Italy wasted
all the energies of the German king.   The aggregate of
fragments was never brought together; the condition
of the whole was only prevented from being anarchy

because there was an absence of any common principle
of rebellion. Every prince did that which was right in
his own eyes, and the emperor looked on and bore it.

IMPORTANT DATES

Frederick II. secures Imperial Crown, 1220.
Frederick goes on a Crusade, 1228
Diet of Worms, 1231.
Frederick returns to Germany, 1235.
Mongol Invasion, 1241-1242.
Innocent IV. excommunicates Frederick, 1245.
William of Holland elected King of Germany, 1247.
Death of Frederick II., 1250.

CHAPTER III

Résumé of German History.—We have now to turn back for the few years which in the last chapter we gave to the view of the last struggles of Frederick and Conrad, to the year 1247, when, after the death of Henry Raspo of Thuringia, the anti-Cæsar, the princes, opposed to the Hohenstaufen or weary of the struggle with the papacy, proceeded to a new election. For from this year, I think, properly dates that long period of German history known as the Interregnum, which is really one of the most important pieces of debatable ground in modern history for its results if not for the signal character of the events that marked it. During this period there was no crowned emperor, nor indeed any one who possessed a full title to the homage of the German kingdom. The two princes who held what there was to hold of power in succession were William, Count of Holland, and Richard, Earl of Cornwall, successively kings of the Romans, but owing to the limited amount of recognition obtained by these princes in the German states, neither of them is regarded as full sovereign or numbered among the emperors. To the imperial title, it is true, they had no title as having never been crowned, but so neither had Rudolf of Hapsburg,

who succeeded them; nor was the papal recognition
awarded to Rudolf in a more signal, although it might
be in a more effective way, than to them.

The Interregnum. — Henry Raspo died in February
1247, having defeated and humiliated Conrad without
having been able to secure a hold on South Germany.
His unexpected death threw the pope and the ecclesiastical party into some perplexity. In the interval between
February and September the crown of Germany was
offered to and refused by several princes of very subordinate importance, both within and without the
empire; at last a young aspirant was found bold
enough to accept: William, Count of Holland, the
descendant of a line of counts which had since the
ninth century ruled the northern portion of Lower
Lorraine in hereditary succession from father to son.
He was twenty years old, and was put forward
chiefly by his uncle, Duke Henry of Brabant, and
the Archbishop of Cologne. The election was transacted as closely under papal directions as that of
Henry Raspo had been, at Neuss, near Cologne, on
October 3. The election is said to have been made by
those princes to whom the right of election belonged,
a subject to which I propose to return by-and-by; but
the actual electors on the occasion were the ecclesiastical
princes. The King of Bohemia and the Margrave of
Brandenburg were present, but their consent cannot
have been given to the election, and the Dukes of
Saxony and Bavaria being in close league with Frederick, were undoubtedly hostile.

In the conflict of authorities it is safest to follow the
probabilities of the case, and to regard the election as
actually carried out by the bishops and princes of Lorraine, the other important personages present contenting

themselves with a passive resistance, which in time to come, if William were successful, might be interpreted as a passive acquiescence. William was knighted preparatory to his coronation, which could not be performed as Aix-la-Chapelle was in possession of the enemy. The first enterprise he undertook was the siege of the imperial city; it was not taken until October 31 in the following year, and on November 1 he was crowned King of the Romans. The year seems to have been productive of success, for the coronation was attended by a much larger concourse of princes than had been present at the election. The fortunes of Conrad and his father were rapidly declining, and Ottocar, King of Bohemia, having his eye fixed on the Austrian possessions bordering on his own dominions, was ready to do his part in expelling the adherents of Hohenstaufen from the south. Still the whole action of William of Holland was confined to the north; nor does he appear more than once south of the line of the Main. He endeavoured by the action of imperial legates to exercise some authority in the districts which he was unable to penetrate in person or with an army, and in the ecclesiastical principalities throughout Germany was to a certain extent recognised. But he was very poor; and his unwise surrender of his own hereditary dominions to his brother left him dependent on the impoverished imperial domains, the revenues of which he had to struggle for with the remains of the Hohenstaufen party. Hence, notwithstanding the destruction or humiliation of that family, William was unable to make himself respected in Germany, and, notwithstanding his own personal claims to valour and judgment, he was treated by the princes, not actually opposed to him, with neglect. Not before Easter 1251, three months after the death of Frederick, was his election confirmed by the pope; and this was probably the consequence of a victory which he obtained over Conrad a few weeks before at Oppenheim.

Anarchy in Germany. — After this battle, Conrad, although he remained half a year longer in Germany, failed to make head against his rival. Germany presented a curious spectacle of two kings, one recognised in the north and the other in the south, each strong enough to prevent his enemy from entering the country that recognised him, but neither strong enough to make good his own position on his own ground. In 1252 he married a daughter of Duke Otto of Brunswick, thus confining his hold on Lower Saxony, and in a way recalling the old organisation of the Welfic party; the same object he attempted to attain by extending the privileges of the house of Brandenburg. But although by these measures he gained perhaps a little wider and more ready recognition, although his abilities as a warrior and a statesman were far from contemptible, he was prevented by his poverty from making even a stroke for the reality of the empire. He was obliged to live very much amongst his relations, and on the scanty revenues which he could obtain by following the pattern of his predecessors in the sale of privileges. His reign is marked by scarcely a single measure of importance, if we except the confederation of the Rhine entered into by the cities and princes for the security of traffic on the river, by the destruction of the castles of the robber or pirate nobles, and the abolition of unjust tolls. This league, which was not able to enforce its objects without recourse to arms, marks the growing importance of the mercantile spirit in the towns on the Rhine, a point to be noted and compared with the advancing power of the Han-

seatic league in the north, which had been formed round
the merchant city of Lübeck during the early part of
the century. The necessities of the emperors had had
this good effect; the privileges they were ready to sell
came into the hands of the men who were best able to
make the most of them; and their policy in promoting
the interest of the towns had a result far more lasting
and far more beneficial than any they had contemplated
when they created it as a counterpoise to the power of
the princes and as a check on their spreading, all-en-
grossing jurisdictions. The league of the Rhine, and
peace between the bishops and the cities, was finally
completed and sanctioned by William at Oppenheim
in 1255.

Deaths of Conrad and William of Holland.—William's
boldest stroke for empire, however, was earlier than
this, and followed his marriage in 1252. After receiving the submission of Saxony and Brandenburg,
he held a diet at Frankfort in June, in which he
declared that Conrad had forfeited the duchy of Swabia,
and passed the same sentence prospectively on all the
vassals of the empire who should not within a year
and a day do homage. But either this was more than
he had power to do, or he wasted his power on other
designs : nearly the whole of the two following years were
spent in war with Flanders, an object certainly not of
imperial policy; that having always been to detach that
county, if possible, from the interests of France. In
1254, after Conrad's death, he revisited Germany, and
then got possession of the strong castle of Trifels and
the insignia of the empire. The cities of the Rhine
again received him with joy, but in the rest of Germany
he had neither authority nor even a show of respect;
he was obliged even to ransom his wife, who had fallen

into the hands of a robber knight of the Palatinate. The state of Germany was anarchy rather than civil war. The reign lasted two years longer. In 1256 William lost his life in an expedition against West Friesland. He is the first of the kings of Germany who comes out of the Lorraine country ; and the characteristics of his reign are in some degree common to all that follow him. He wanted money and he wanted connection. No one was closely allied with him except the pope and the prelates. He would be regarded by the Germans of Upper Germany as hardly a German prince at all; none of his ancestors had taken part in the struggles or successes of Germany : they were brave men, crusaders, faithful for the most part to the imperial throne which protected them but gave them very little trouble in the way of interference ; but their states were comparatively insignificant, and lay far too much on one side of Germany. William, I think, has been hardly treated in general by German writers as a mere papal pretender : he was certainly a brave man and had some talent for government, but he was poor and ill supported, and not a likely man to undo the mischief of the last fifty years. He was only twenty-nine when he died. His children were too young to assert a claim even if their friends had been foolish enough to advocate their inheritance of trouble and labour.

The death of William left Germany without even a nominal head. Conrad had died two years before, leaving the Hohenstaufen influence in Germany at zero. Conradin was two years old when his father died, but Swabia was already lost and rapidly being broken up among the petty lords, whom the removal of their duke rendered independent. The forfeiture decreed by William strengthened the hands of these, although it was powerless so far as it might have tended to the consolidation of his own power. Why could not Germany, now having got rid of the rival kings, and being pledged in common to no particular policy, have done as was done sixteen years after, and joined to elect a ruler who would be at the least a rallying-point for the friends of order? Whatever may have been the cause, and there were many no doubt at work among the different interests of the kingdom, no such attempt, *bonâ fide*, was made. No doubt the papal party had much to do with this: it was necessary to prevent even the possibility of a reaction in favour of the Hohenstaufens, or the election of an emperor who was even remotely implicated in their policy. But none of the princes was ambitious of a crown so impoverished, or liable to such inveterate evils as those which had embittered the existence of the last wearers of it.

Election of Richard of Cornwall and of Alfonso, 1257.—But whatever were the thoughts and intentions of the influential men, the business of the nation must proceed: matters, bad as they were, were not ripe for the abolition of the central authority and the absolute division of Germany amongst a crowd of independent princes. As there was now no emperor, nor king of the Romans, nor even a pretender to the title, nor even a person designated to the succession—a thing which had not occurred more than once or twice since the extinction of the Karolings—the assembly of the princes must be held in due course to elect some one; and such was the reluctance of all to undertake the task that not even parties were formed for the election of particular persons until the electors met on the

Epiphany of 1257 to make their election. Therein and about Frankfort assembled the Archbishop of Cologne, the Count Palatine, and Duke of Bavaria with his brother Henry, outside the city, and the Archbishop of Trèves and the Duke of Saxony in the city. The Archbishop of Mainz, the only person wanting to make up the tale of the clerical electors, was in prison at Brunswick, but he sent his proxy to the Archbishop of Cologne; the King of Bohemia and the Margrave of Brandenburg communicated their intention by letters. But all hopes of a peaceful election were defeated by the conduct of the Archbishop of Trèves, who, in concert with the Duke of Saxony, refused to allow the other two present electors to enter the city. On the Octaves of the Epiphany, the Archbishop of Cologne and the Count Palatine elected Richard of Cornwall, brother of Henry III. of England; but to this the Archbishop of Trèves and the Duke of Saxony refused their consent: they fortified themselves by delay, and with the letters of the absent electors, and on Palm Sunday announced that their choice had fallen on Alfonso X., King of Castile.

It would be vain to speculate on the causes of this extraordinary election in any idea of attaining even a probable solution. Even Milman is obliged to put down the choice of Richard of Cornwall to the ambition of the Archbishop of Cologne, who, he thinks, was desirous of ruling the empire as the agent and with the wealth of Richard. But if this explains one side, what can explain the other? The electors of Alfonso were struck, we are told, with his reputation for wisdom. Possibly so; but all that he did to justify that reputation in German matters was that he had the wisdom to keep out of the way.

Richard was not so wise; he hastened to the scene of action, and was crowned with his wife at Aix-la-Chapelle on Ascension Day. Alfonso, to whom the imperial insignia had been sent by Frederick, Duke of Lorraine, promised to come as soon as he could, but never fulfilled the promise. The question of the disputed election was carried to Rome; there Pope Alexander IV., regarding the conduct of the Archbishop of Trèves as illegal, and as voiding the election in which he took part, gave sentence in 1259. He is said to have inclined to Richard's side, and even to have recognised his election as valid. But it would appear that there is a doubt of the genuineness of the letters in which this recognition was accorded. Richard is known more familiarly in English than in German history as King of the Romans and Richard of Almain. Observe for a moment Richard's connection with Germany: in the first place he was brother-in-law of Frederick II., who had married his sister, the Empress Isabella; he was also own cousin to the Emperor Otto IV., the son of Henry the Lion; if the name of Welf and Waibeling still bore any signification in Germany, Richard may have had friends on both sides; but on the other hand he was brother of King Henry, who had just accepted for his son, Edmund of Lancaster, the kingdom of Sicily, the inheritance of Conradin; and he was also brother-in-law of Charles of Anjou, the destined exterminator of the Hohenstaufen rule in Naples.

Richard of Cornwall's Character.—It is a common mistake in historians, both English and German, to regard Richard as a vain, foolish person, very rich, and easily prevailed on to waste his money for the mere purposes of personal vanity. It was very far otherwise in his own time. In England he was regarded as

D

more politic than honest : as a tricky, deceptive man ; but
not as a fool by any means.   I think, however, that this is
too low an estimate of him : judged by the line he took
in both French and English matters, he seems to have
been decidedly an able politician.   He was an advocate
of peace when his foolish brother would fain have
carried on a fruitless war ; he more than once interfered to prevent quarrels that must have embittered
the already exasperated condition of parties ; until he
was provoked by the opposition of Simon de Montfort
he was always on the side of a conciliatory policy
towards the barons, and although very unpopular from
his wealth and foreign connections, was by no means
opposed to proper concessions to the popular demands.
He refused to lend his brother money ; but that, to my
mind, remembering what sort of a man in money
matters Henry III. was, is a strong proof of wisdom.

It is to be noted that both Richard and Alfonso
were directly descended from Henry II. of England,
who had been accused of aspiring to the empire for
himself, and closely related, therefore, with Otto IV.,
his grandson.   Although Richard's election was far
from unanimous and his recognition far from universal, he had no difficulty in obtaining and retaining
the measure of recognition which he did obtain.   No
obstacle was offered to his coronation or to his authority
where it was at all admitted, nor did any one appeal to
arms against him.   The absence of the rival king, the
strong pressure put by the popes on their supporters
to take part in no measure that could result in the
revival of the Hohenstaufen interest, and the fact that
practical independence was secured to the princes by
the merely nominal rule of such a sovereign ; the dislike of French influence, which had been employed, it

was said, on behalf of Alfonso, although at an earlier period Louis IX. had refused to join the pope against Frederick and Conrad—all these things conspired to give Richard an easy, if an expensive time of it.

Gradually the princes who had supported Alfonso, notably the King of Bohemia, who indeed was ready to support any one who would support him in his claims to Austria, came in and acknowledged Richard, making use of his necessities to obtain from him the recognition or extension of their privileges. From the pope he never obtained a formal act of recognition or sentence in his favour against Alfonso. Alexander IV. left the matter undecided ; Urban IV. summoned the competitors to Rome, but as neither of them attended, the suit still hung in suspense ; Clement IV., without acknowledging Richard, refused to acknowledge Alfonso ; and before Gregory X. had made up his mind, Richard died.

The Extent of his Influence.—The immediate influence of Richard in Germany, like that of his predecessor, was confined to the Rhine valley, the Palatinate, and the bishoprics of Cologne and Mainz. He was less supported than William had been on the Netherland and French side, for there lay the strength of William's family connections, and the influence of France had not yet been given to a rival candidate. But one of the few royal or imperial acts performed by Alfonso was to invest Frederick of Lorraine, who had brought him the news of the election, with that duchy ; and it marks the weakness of Richard or the strength of the Archbishop of Trèves, that he was able to maintain his hold upon a principality so near the seat of government. Nor did Richard possess, as William had done, the interest of the Church party in South Germany, which acted in strict obedience to the papal movements, and as the popes did, abstained from taking a side in the struggle, if struggle it can be called. But, on the other hand, Richard in the long run obtained a far more extensive recognition, and executed more important acts of sovereignty than either William or Conrad, and he possessed a source of strength which they were without, namely, money. I do not wish to exaggerate the importance of Richard's reign; but owing to his close connection with England we may be allowed to bestow rather more than a mere passing attention upon it. I have mentioned some of the events of the English part of his life which lead to the conclusion that his ability has been underrated by historians generally. This is easily accounted for. In England Richard was unpopular with both parties; he refused to minister, without security, to the extravagance of Henry III., and he opposed, both on political, and more still on personal grounds, the policy of Simon de Montfort. By the royalists he was regarded as spending his wealth in pursuit of a shadow of foreign dominion; by the popular party as a trickster and as a sharer in the oppressions and exactions of the government. The French historians hate him as they do everything English; and the Germans, always prone to the same feeling, were only too glad to be able to justify their contempt of him, by the mean opinion of his own countrymen. The facts, although they are far from making Richard a great man or a great king, give a different impression from any of these opinions. In the absence of any strong opposition Richard must have had some stronger recommendation than his money, or money must have been more powerful in Germany than is compatible with the honour and greatness of the nation.

His Title of King of Germany justified.—We will now look at the extent of the dominion which recognised him. In the first place, of course, the territories of Mainz and Cologne do so; in the second, Bavaria and the Palatinate. These were the estates which joined in the election. But the condition of things was different. Mainz and Cologne might, as Milman says, expect to reign through Richard; but Lewis, Duke of Bavaria and Count Palatine, was the brother of Elizabeth, the widow of King Conrad, and in Bavaria, at Landshut, under her brother's protection, the little Conradin was being educated by his mother for his brilliant but short career. The sentence of William of Holland had indeed dismembered the duchy of Swabia, but had not been able to secure the alienation of the hereditary estates of Conradin, and from them, under the protection of his uncle, funds were drawn for him which were enough to maintain a child of seven or eight years old in all necessary splendour. The hostility of the popes was unrelaxing, and it is perhaps owing to this apparent toleration of Conradin, whose election to the kingdom they were most anxious to prevent, that we are to ascribe their reluctance to recognise Richard. In the north of Germany Richard probably had sufficient family interest to keep his hold on his cousins of Brunswick; the Margrave of Brandenburg, who had voted for Alfonso, was shortly bought over. The Archbishop of Trèves, by the mediation of France, made peace with Richard; and Austria, being torn in pieces by her neighbours of Bavaria and Bohemia, had no representative but the boy Frederick, the sharer of the exploits and of the fate of Conradin.

Richard's authority, although superficial, was very widely recognised, so widely, in fact, as to vindicate his

title as King of Germany completely. The number of
diplomatic acts of his which are preserved show that every
important prince in Germany paid him the compliment
of getting some privilege or other from him : his grants
to the free towns, who, of course, had themselves to give
effect to his grants, for it was little but parchment and
paper that they could expect of him, show a decided
advancement in German life of the important elements
of municipal and mercantile independence and the
measures taken for the promotion of the interests of
the Hanseatic league, especially in relation to England,
prove that Richard either by his own mother-wit or
under the advice of sound German counsellors, was
ready to work his influence with his brother Henry
for the common benefit of their respective subjects.
It was in 1260 that Henry III., under the pressure of
his brother, granted to all the merchants of Germany
in connection with the Hanseatic league the same
mercantile privileges in England which had been
bestowed on the burghers of Cologne by Henry II.
On the connection of the Hanse towns with England,
it would be as well to read the clever little essay of
Dr. Pauli in his "Pictures of Old England."

Summary of Richard's Position.—To sum up, then.
Richard was not a party king in Germany: he was
recognised all through the country and by every
element of society, although that recognition involved no authority or jurisdiction: he was in league
with both Guelf and Ghibelline; the pope refused
the recognition that the Church, the princes, and
the towns accorded; his acts, so far as they can be
interpreted as showing his intentional policy, were
of a wise and provident character: he made few
enemies, and he had no battles to fight. His position

was a difficult one in many ways: it was from his English estates that he drew the money, which was, of course, the foundation and strength of his influence in Germany. To neglect England would be to sacrifice both the substance and the shadow of power. It is absurd to talk of him, as the German writers do, as preferring inglorious ease in England to vindicating his rights by arms in Germany. His position in England was anything but easy, inglorious as it may have been. His position in Germany was easy, whether or no it could be called glorious. But if he had neglected England, he would have lost all.

It does not belong to German history to apologise for the part that he took in the great constitutional struggle: perhaps a fairer idea of his position in Germany may give to us a clearer notion of the reasons why he took the side he did in English politics, but I cannot do more than indicate it here. No effort that he could have made in Germany without the revenues of his English estates could have maintained or improved his position, for he had not an inch of hereditary property in the empire, and so far was in a worse position than William of Holland.

Fighting in England for his county of Cornwall, he fought really for his German kingdom. It may have been unwise in him to court or to accept the election, but that once done, I do not see that he is to blame for taking the best means he could take to maintain it. He made, during the fifteen years which his nominal reign contained, four visits to Germany. The first immediately after his election extends from April 1257 to January 1259, and includes nearly two years. During those years he was crowned at Aix-la-Chapelle, and very considerably strengthened the position of the free cities, Cologne, Frankfort, Nuremberg, and others; he repealed the act of forfeiture passed by William of Holland against Margaret of Flanders, and made himself new friends in South Germany. In January 1259 he revisited England, where, we must remember, he was obliged to swear to observe the Provisions of Oxford at his landing: he remained here, however, only until June. From June to October he spent in Germany, principally in the Palatinate; his principal acts show him busy in acquiring the friendship of the Swabian nobles and the princes of the Upper Rhine. From October 1259 to June 1262 he was again in England, supporting Henry III. against Simon de Montfort in that sudden and partly successful attempt made, without the co-operation of Prince Edward, and in contempt of the oath taken by the king, to upset the Provisions of Oxford.

Henry left England for France at the same time as Richard's third departure for Germany. This third visit lasted from July 1262 to February 1263. The most important act of it was the admission of Ottocar of Bohemia to the duchy of Austria and Styria, for which he had been struggling for many years, and which he was to forfeit under the next reign. He also declared Zürich a free city of the empire during this visit, an act which, as opposed to the policy of the dukes of Swabia, may be held to mark a step in advance to Swiss independence. In this visit we find amongst his allies the new Archbishop of Trèves. On the 10th of February 1263 he returned to England, where he shared with Henry in the great events of the Barons' War; fought and was taken prisoner at Lewes in 1264, and was released in September 1265 after the battle of

Evesham. This time he remained five years away from Germany, and indeed only revisited it in 1268. It is to this long interval that the short career of Conradin belongs. In other respects Germany seems to have done fairly well without her king.

History and Death of Conradin.—Conradin had been living in Bavaria whilst Manfred was fighting the battle of the family in Italy. Manfred's policy was to disconnect the Sicilian heritage of Frederick from the odium and danger of the German connection; and with this view he had allowed himself to be elected King of the Sicilies, in the full intention, we may believe, of making his nephew Conradin his heir. But the popes were determined to destroy the Hohenstaufen in every shape and form, and would no more tolerate Manfred as elective King of the Sicilies, which they claimed as a fief of the Holy See, than they would tolerate the child Conradin as a possible candidate for the kingdom of Germany or for the empire. The hostility which had begun in the politics of Innocent III. and Honorius III. had developed, in Innocent IV. and Alexander IV., into the bitterest personal hatred; and in Italy generally the quarrels of Guelf and Ghibelline seemed to advance in venomous and personal hatred as the origins of the names and of the quarrels became matters of antiquarian research.

In February 1265, at the battle of Benevento, Manfred fell before the cruel and vindictive Charles of Anjou, the papal hostility following the brilliant son of Frederick even into his grave. Conradin, the last hope of the Ghibelline party, was now only thirteen years old. Charles had an interval of two years allowed him, during which he showed all the cruelty and oppressiveness of his disposition, and proved himself the worthy pro-

genitor of a line of kings whose name is synonymous
with oppression and bloodshed. In 1267 Conradin
was summoned from Bavaria. He had, by the assistance of his maternal kinsmen, and by the sale of his last
allods to Lewis of Bavaria and Meinhard of Tyrol, his
stepfather, and his friend Frederick of Baden, the last
claimant of the honours of the Babenberg dukes of
Austria whom Ottocar had ousted, collected a force
of about 4000 Germans. With these he crossed the
Alps, and was everywhere welcomed as a deliverer.

The pope was frantic ; he summoned Conradin before
him at Viterbo ; he ordered Ottocar to seize the
relics of Conradin's Swabian possessions, the remnant
of the Welfic allods bequeathed by Duke Welf to
Frederick Barbarossa ; he raised Charles of Anjou to
the title of Peacemaker throughout Tuscany and all the
provinces of the Roman empire. From Verona, early
in 1268, Conradin, at the head of a Ghibelline army,
advanced towards Rome, and passed, within sight of the
pope, the walls of Viterbo. At Rome senate and people
welcomed him ; but the military skill and discipline of
the French were too much for him. At the battle of
Tagliacozzo both Conradin and Frederick of Austria
were taken, and after a mock trial, in contravention of
all national law and morality, were beheaded at Naples.
So perished together the last heirs of the great Swabian
dynasty, for it was through Agnes of Swabia, the daughter
of Henry IV., that the ancestors of both Conrad and
Frederick inherited the ancient blood of the imperial
line. With them the older medieval empire seems to
lose its last breath of vitality. In Germany it may be
regarded as extinct after the death of Frederick.

Death of Richard of Cornwall, 1272.—The position of
Richard, however, was little affected by the tragic

events taking place in Italy. He was growing old, in fact, although not so much in years as in habits; he had led an active and adventurous life, and was amusing himself at Berkhamstead as well as he could, nobody much missing him in Germany. Three years after his release from imprisonment he reappeared in his kingdom, September 1268, and this time he stayed long enough to transact another (the third) courtship and marriage. The lady was the very beautiful Beatrice of Falkenstein, the daughter of Philip, the chamberlain of the emperor and guardian of the castle of Trifels, which held the imperial ornaments. As soon as his marriage was over, and the marriage seems to have been nearly all that he did effect on the visit, he returned to England, where he lived nearly three years longer, chiefly at Berkhamstead. He died about six months before his brother, Henry III., on April 2, 1272, before he had had time to try whether the newly elected pope would acquiesce in the abeyance of the imperial authority, but not before he had heard of the cruel murder of his son, Henry of Almain, by the two sons of Simon de Montfort, which was perpetrated at Viterbo on the occasion of the election of Pope Gregory X.

IMPORTANT DATES

Death of Conrad IV., 1254.
Death of William of Holland, 1256.
Richard of Cornwall and Alfonso of Castile
    elected emperors, 1256.
The Interregnum, 1256–1273.
Death of Conradin, 1268.
Death of Richard of Cornwall, 1272.

CHAPTER IV

The year 1272—Political situation in Germany—The rise of new
families in Germany—The Princes—The Diet—Imperial elections
—The electors—Rudolf of Hapsburg—His election as emperor—
His reign—His relations with Burgundy and England.

The Importance of 1272.—The year 1272 forms the era
of an entirely new epoch of German history. We
may say that, during the twenty-two years which had
now passed since the death of Frederick II., the air
had been clearing; the forces of the old system, as
it had existed from the days of Otto the First to
the fall of the Hohenstaufen, its families and parties,
had waned and died away; the accession of a pope,
Gregory X., in September 1271, who was determined
to set things on a better footing, coincided with the
removal of that ostensible head of the kingdom whose
title had held good in default of any other being put
forward that was not manifestly absurd. The passing
away of the shadow of empire in the person of Richard
of Cornwall (April 1272), left the empire in a condition
in which it had not been since the time of Charles the
Great. Strictly elective as was the crown of the German
kingdom, and stricter still as was the electoral theory,
after the time that the imperial crown became permanently connected with it, we cannot fail to observe
that the claims of descent, and relationship to some one
of the imperial families, had been in nearly every case
regarded as a qualification second only to personal
fitness.

The Question of the Succession.—Actually, though not in theory perhaps, the plan of choosing the selection of the late king who was fittest for the position, whenever a direct heir was wanting, the custom that was recognised in England under the Anglo-Saxon kings, and which is traceable even on the accession of John, had been acted upon. Conrad of Franconia and Otto of Saxony, who competed for the crown after the death of Lewis the Child, were both connected, or had the reputation of being connected, with the Karolings. The Saxon dynasty lasted for four generations, the form of election being gone through although son succeeded father. Henry II. succeeded his cousin Otto as elect sovereign, and Conrad the Salic succeeded Henry II.; in both cases the title rested on relationship as well as on the choice of the people. From Conrad the Salic the crown descends down to Henry V., *hereditarily*, and after the one break in the person of Lothair II., it again reverts to the descendants of Henry IV., in whom the representation continues until the extinction of the Hohenstaufen.

With Conradin, in 1268, died also Frederick of Austria, who was descended in the same way from Henry IV., and in whom ended likewise that great line of the Babenberg dukes and margraves, whose feud with the Franconian dukes is the first clear fact of post-Karolingian history. The whole representation of the royal house was extinct, and there remained not one person in Germany itself who possessed anything like a hereditary recommendation. But not only so. There remained not one great house of the rank which had formerly furnished candidates for the kingdom. The families of the great duchies of old were extinct or dwindled down to insignificance. The great Welfic house, which had once reigned from the Eyder to the Po and the Tiber, were contented with the little principality that Frederick II. had created for it out of the remains of its allodial property in Lower Saxony. The Wittelsbachs in Bavaria dated but from the forfeiture of Henry the Lion in 1180, the power of the house of Brandenburg, and the ducal house of Saxony, dated from the same. Swabia and Franconia, long in a state of subdivision and confusion, lost even their titular head in Conradin, and Austria was approaching the condition of dismemberment among rival claimants. No German prince aspired to the crown, or was even willing to take it, when William of Holland, still less when Richard of England, was elected. The old things had quite passed away. Germany was no longer the aggregate of the five nations, who had elected Henry the Fowler and the Ottos; and the central diet, with its rough division of estates, and its mass of conflicting dignities, was a very different, less imposing, but more practically intractable body than the ancient councils of the nations.

The Origin of the Nobility in Germany.—There was a new system of nobility immensely more numerous than the old, and it is necessary to get an idea how these new families and new interests originated.

It is scarcely necessary to premise that they emerged to power by the extinction and dismemberment of the great duchies; the question is, how came they to be in such a position as to take advantage of those extinctions? There were three possible origins of nobility— ancient allodial inheritance, the position of imperial functionaries, and the erection of feudal territorial jurisdictions. These three often, as in Saxony, combined in one family or person; but, in all cases where that was not so, there were always two classes of competitors for any vacancy produced by the extinction of the third. The five nations were originally governed by dukes; and under these dukes the whole country was divided into *gaus* or shires, as we would call them, each of which had its count. The office of duke was in theory a military one; that of count, or *graf*, a judicial one; but not only did they very naturally become confounded, but the offices, of course, fell so naturally to the most powerful allodial owner in each division, that they quickly became hereditary and feudal. They might be feudally subject to the duke, or feudally dependent on the King of Germany directly, or they might hold lands and dignities, as was the case in England, by a multitude of titles and tenures of different sorts. When, then, a great duchy became extinct, there were always a large number of counts ready to assert their independence, or to compete for the vacancy. When Swabia and Franconia were extinguished, every little landowner, who had held of the dukes before, became immediate, and had all the privileges of a tenant in chief. But, besides the great duchies, there were on the outskirts of the kingdom a number of marks, or margraviates, only inferior in size and dignity to duchies, and, in the interstices between the duchies, the debatable ground once occupied by little tribes not absorbed into the duchies, were one or two landgraviates or provincial countships, which in their turn rose with the fall of the duchies. And in the third place, there was a sort of official nobility, whose original business was to look after the imperial interests in the duchies, and who bore the title of Count Palatine. These Counts Palatine were often established by the emperors, as a counterbalance to the power of the hereditary dukes, and very naturally stepped into the places left vacant by the extinction of

the ducal houses. Thus, in Bavaria, was the Count of
Scheyren, the lord of Wittelsbach and Palatine, who,
after the forfeiture of Henry the Lion, became Duke of
Bavaria. The Count Palatine of Saxony was the Landgrave of Thuringia, then the Margrave of Meissen,
ultimately the dignity became attached to the dukedom
and electorate of Saxony in the house of Wettin.
So, on the extinction or absorption of Franconia, the
Count Palatine of Franconia succeeded to the place and
influence of the old duke ; and this was the only County
Palatine which, not sinking its honours in a superior
title, descended to the present century in that form, and
gave name to two extensive territories, the Upper and
Lower Palatinates.

The German Diet.—Out of these materials the German
diets of the new period were composed ; the bond of
union being a common interest rather than any cohesion
of organisation, and the old causes of division existing
still in their fullest extent. Swabian counts, for instance,
might be constantly warring against one another, but
they were not brought a whit nearer in feeling or interest
to Saxon or Bavarian counts, merely because the representative integrity of the old nation was lost sight of.

Besides the princes, the diets contained the prelates
and the towns, the latter of which were by their representatives just now acquiring the position, a sufficiently
humble one, with which they had to be content. The great
privilege, the highest dignity, both lay and ecclesiastical,
consisted of the right of voting for a king of Germany ;
a point which brings us up to the moment which we
are discussing.

The Imperial Elections.—The early kings were elected
by the assemblies of the nations, either conjointly or
separately, Bavaria, Saxony, Swabia, Franconia, and

Lorraine. But where the hereditary principle had been so largely admitted, and the sovereign was allowed to nominate his successor before his death, there was obviously a probability that the right of voting would become vested in the persons of the chiefs of the nations; would become an honorary privilege seldom used, and, when used under such limitations, likely to be used without any very precise or uniform show of legality. In the election that followed the death of Henry V., the votes seem to have been given by the dukes rather than by the nations, and by the dukes, archbishops, and princes without any very distinct idea as to the foundation of the right of voting. They chose ten persons out of their number, who, as in ecclesiastical elections, by compromise, prætaxed or chose a king, whose election was afterwards formally accepted. I suppose it will never now be exactly determined how the number of electors became restricted to seven, three spiritual and four temporal, but the fact that it did, when so limited, vest itself in the particular seven may have been owing to their filling the several honorary offices of the imperial household. The three archbishops were the arch-chancellors, and the four lay electors were cupbearer, steward, marshal, and chamberlain. These offices had been attached to Bohemia, the County Palatine, Saxony, and Brandenburg for a long period, although perhaps not permanently so until the reign of Frederick Barbarossa, A.D. 1184. The lay electorates represent, we see, the imperial jurisdiction in the Count Palatine, the feudal in the King of Bohemia, the national in the Duke of Saxony, and the margraviate element in Brandenburg. We miss the ancient nations, Bavaria, Swabia, and Franconia, but we must remember that the Palatine of the Rhine now

E

represented Franconia, and that, when the system received its final form, Bavaria was held by the same person, Lewis of Wittelsbach. These persons conducted the election of Henry Raspe, William of Holland, and Richard of Cornwall ; and although the first mention of them as the seven electors is found in the documents relating to the controversy between Richard and Alfonso, the existence of a set of electors, who most probably were these seven, is proved by the mention of the dignity in the diploma by which Frederick Barbarossa founded the duchy of Austria.

The Election of Rudolf of Hapsburg, 1273.—The machinery, then, for an election fortunately existed, having been tried in the three last nominations ; and the extinction of the old houses, the duchies, and the nations did not leave the kingdom at the mercy of the popes. The throne was vacant for more than a year before the new election. Richard died in April 1272, and it was not until Michaelmas 1273 that the electors met at Frankfort with the rest of the princes, at the urgent pressure of Gregory X. The electors were Werner, Archbishop of Mainz, Engelbert of Falkenburg, Archbishop of Cologne, Henry of Winstingen, Archbishop of Trèves, Lewis of Wittelsbach, the Count Palatine, Albert of Ballenstadt, Duke of Saxony, the Margrave of Brandenburg, and Henry of Wittelsbach, brother of the Count Palatine, and Duke of Bavaria, who voted instead of Ottocar, King of Bohemia. There were no candidates for the crown, unless we call Ottocar of Bohemia one ; but, as no one voted for him, he may be left out. Count Meinhard of Tyrol declared that the crown must fall on either Bernhard of Carinthia, Albert of Goritz, his own brother, or Rudolf of Hapsburg. No great prince was willing to accept, as before. At length it was determined that Lewis of Wittelsbach, the Count Palatine, should make the election. He accepted the task, and on the following day announced that his choice was Rudolf, Count of Hapsburg. The King of Bohemia was of course much disgusted; the Archbishop of Mainz, Rudolf's patron, proportionately delighted. Fortunately the electoral number could be made up without King Ottocar, and the election was formally transacted. On the 24th of the same October he was crowned at Aix-la-Chapelle King of the Romans.

The First Hapsburg Emperor.—There suddenly comes on the stage—so suddenly that but for their subsequent history, none would have cared perhaps to investigate their former lot—that famous family which ever since has occupied the first rank in Germany, and in Europe generally, which has governed as wide a European empire as Charles the Great, besides the new world of America, and has gone nearer than any other in Christendom to realise the idea of universal empire.

Rudolf was a noble adventurer, who, in a subordinate capacity, had taken part in all the wars of Germany since Frederick's time. He was heir of the county of Hapsburg in the Aargau; the ruins of his paternal castle lie on the right as you go from Olten to Zurich, about halfway. By his marriage with Gertrude of Hohenberg, he obtained a great estate in addition to his hereditary claims, in Alsace, and partly by war, partly by inheritance, increased his paternal domain.

In the war that followed the death of Frederick, Rudolf had ranged himself on the side of Conrad, and in that connection had risen to the office of Marshal of the Court to Ottocar, King of Bohemia. From Bohemia he had come back to Alsace, and had been elected general of the Strassburgers in their war against their bishops from 1261-1269. He afterwards filled the same office in connection with the town of Zürich, at the head of whose citizens he humbled and defeated the proud Count of Regensberg. Later we find him leading one of the factions of the city of Basel against the bishop of that place, and it was whilst besieging Basel, then in the hands of the bishop's party, that he was elected King of the Romans. Curiously enough, the person who brought him the diploma of election was Frederick of Zollern, burgrave of Nuremberg, the first famous ancestor of the kings of Prussia ; thus at the same moment spring into light the two great families whose parties, religious principles, and alliances were so many ages after, and for so many ages, to divide Germany, and indeed Europe between them. Rudolf's acquaintance with Archbishop Werner of Mainz is said to have begun when the latter was once travelling through Switzerland to Rome, and was entertained on the way and guided through the horrors of the mountains by Rudolf. The jest, which is said to have passed at the election, that Rudolf had six daughters to give away in marriage among those princes who wanted to rise to fortune, is curious, compared with what was the actual so well known fortune of his house. The Hapsburgs, in every case, gained by marriage, instead of laying the foundation of new families by bestowing their daughters. The first example was the acquisition of the Alsatian estates of Hohenburg, the marriage of Rudolf himself. But of this hereafter.

Rudolf's Character.—Rudolf was not of the highest type of a deliverer, but he was a good king, and a man could be in those days hardly a good king who did not manage to keep on fair terms with the pope. He was also a prudent man, bent on exacting and increasing the influence of the family which he was founding, and this is a policy which constitutes the entire religion, principle, and political programme during the whole period of its growth. Rudolf did consent to make concessions to the pope in Italy, which strengthened his own position in Germany. The antecedents of Rudolf were not such as make a man a hero, who has not been born one : the empire which he governed he found at the very depth of dismemberment and dis-organisation. The empire he founded was not one of the highest order of empires, but it was a fairly safe one, and had the merit of living much longer than any that had preceded it. The principle that he represented, the cordial union of the imperial and papal interests, was one which had not been successfully tried before. It had been attempted by the Saxon emperors, who had both to reform and to protect the papacy, and the Saxon interest —that is, the North German—had been ever since dis-tinctly papal. But the South German dynasties, the Fran-conian and the Swabian, whose personal interests brought them nearer Italy and Rome, had never been able to keep on even peaceful terms with the popes, the North German alliance of the latter acting rather as a dividing than as a consolidating force. But the house of Austria ruling, either by possession or by influence, the whole of South Germany, has almost always—always in fact, until the accession of Charles V. brought up again the old Neapolitan difficulty that had been fatal to the Hohenstaufens—continued to be hand and glove with Rome.

His Accession an Epoch in German History.—More important, perhaps—at all events in view of the life of the German people—is the fact that from this time we seem to start a principle the reverse of that

which has hitherto guided us.   Up to this time we have
to keep our attention fixed on the disintegration of
Germany—both the internal causes of disruption and
the external forces of divulsion.   Henceforth we have to
watch the process of aggregation, the uniting of estates
and consolidation by external agencies: a process exemplified on the largest scale by Austria and Prussia,
but not the less going on in most of the other principalities, and destined to marshal a consolidated North
and South against one another.

One of Rudolf's first acts after his coronation was to
bestow three of his six daughters on the three lay
electors who had supported him, Lewis the Count
Palatine, Albert of Saxony, and Otto of Brandenburg.
The other three afterwards married to the consolidation of the family interest.   The next step was to obtain
papal recognition.   Gregory X. held in 1274 the Council
of Lyons.   To this Alfonso of Castile and Ottocar of
Bohemia both sent ambassadors to ask for the empire.
The pope, who had perhaps some occult share in the
election of Rudolf, only held back until he had made
his terms.   Rudolf surrendered to him the Romagna,
the exarchate, the inheritance of the Countess Matilda,
and much else, all in fact that the pope required, to
be held in full sovereignty, together with the suzerainty
of Sicily, Sardinia, and Corsica.   The voice of history
calls this inglorious and mercenary; I think that Rudolf
was, as a German prince, wise to keep clear of Italy at
any cost.   The bargain being concluded, Gregory came
as far as Lausanne to meet the king, and there bestowed
his benediction on the 18th of October 1275.   Rudolf
then undertook to go to Rome to be crowned emperor,
after which he was to conduct a crusade to Palestine.
Neither of these promises were ever fulfilled; and

Gregory X., who was a sincere sort of pope, having complained to Rudolf of his broken faith, proceeded so far as to excommunicate him; and left him, it is said, excommunicated at his own death in 1276.

Rudolf and Ottocar of Bohemia.—Rudolf preferred, however, negotiating to fighting or visiting Italy, and in 1278 he obtained absolution from Nicolas III. by the gift of the city of Bologna and its appurtenances. The negotiations on this point are tedious, and concern Germany but little. The greatest war which Rudolf engaged in, after his succession, was that with his old enemy, Ottocar of Bohemia, which ended in his acquiring for his family the whole of the duchy of Austria. Austria had lost its last duke in the direct line of the Babenberg house in 1246, Frederick the Warlike, the old enemy and afterwards the last left friend of Frederick II. His inheritance, or the claim to it, devolved on his niece Gertrude. Her husband Uladislas, Margrave of Moravia, succeeded, in despite of the emperor and several rival claimants, in getting possession of the duchy, but died without issue the next year; and Gertrude conveyed her claims to her second husband, Hermann of Baden, by whom she was the mother of Duke Frederick, who perished with Conradin at Naples in 1268. Hermann received the investiture of the duchy from William of Holland, and maintained himself in possession for three years, when Gertrude was left again a widow.

Her third husband, a Russian prince named Romanus, failed to make good his claims, and from that time the duchy fell a prey to rival competitors, the most formidable of whom were Ottocar, Margrave of Moravia, son of Wenzel, King of Bohemia, and the Duke of Bavaria. Ottocar strengthened the claim which he had originally by the offer of the estates of Austria themselves, by marrying a sister of Frederick the Warlike, Margaret, widow of Henry, the unfortunate King of the Romans, son of Frederick II. He divorced her in 1261. He got possession of the duchy of Austria about 1252, Styria falling to the Duke of Bavaria. To Moravia and Austria, Ottocar added in 1253 by inheritance the kingdom of Bohemia, and in 1269 Carinthia, by a treaty of succession with Ulric, the last duke, excluding his brother Philip. This made him the most powerful prince in Germany, and, in conjunction with his overbearing and quarrelsome disposition, prevented him from obtaining the great object of his ambition, the imperial crown. He was no mean antagonist for King Rudolf, who as yet had little more to depend on than his own estates in Switzerland and Alsace. Ottocar refused to recognise Rudolf as king, and Rudolf determined to listen to the complaints which poured into his court from the Austrians against their duke, and against the Duke Henry of Bavaria, who had now taken part with his aggressive neighbour.

After long negotiations, persuasions, and threats, Rudolf succeeded in detaching Duke Henry from the alliance, though not before both he and Ottocar had been declared enemies of the empire in a diet at Augsburg. Rudolf's task was not an easy one; he had, before he could undertake a war of any importance, to put down the robber counts of Swabia, with whom he had formerly mixed on terms of equality. This occupied him all 1275; he then reconciled the Duke of Bavaria by a marriage of his son with another daughter of his own, and at last, in 1276, invaded Austria, and besieged Vienna. The armies met with purpose of battle, but, before a blow was struck, Ottocar, sensible that his conduct had surrounded him with treason, submitted to Rudolf, and surrendered to him Austria, Styria, Carniola, and Carinthia, consenting to hold Bohemia and Moravia as fiefs of the empire (November 1276). The arrangement was to be strengthened by a double marriage; but Ottocar did not keep faith. Rudolf continued in Austria, strengthening his personal interest there, and galling the pride of Ottocar.

In 1278 Ottocar renewed the war, and in a battle, fought on the Marchfeld before Vienna on August 26, Rudolf was completely victorious. Ottocar perished in the fight, leaving as his representative a child of twelve years old, named Wenzel. The great enemy was thus got rid of, and peace so far as he was concerned was secured; but there remained the distribution of the spoils, and the fulfilment of Rudolf's most necessary policy, the engrossing of the largest portion of them in his own family.

The Duchy of Alemannia.—Before proceeding to say how this was determined, it is necessary to look back on the former history of the states which come into great prominence for the first time in German history in connection with the house of Hapsburg. The two southern nations of Germany were the Alemanni and the Bavarians—the Alemanni reaching from the Rhine and Burgundy to the river Lech, and the Bavarians from the Lech to Hungary.

The duchy of Alemannia, sometimes a kingdom, and sometimes divided into two large portions, had less coherence than any of the German duchies, and was subject after the Karoling times to more changes of dynasty. The mountains and lakes of Switzerland were an obstacle to its being ever well compacted, and much more so was the independent spirit of the inhabitants. Nor were the limits between Alemannia and the

Burgundian kingdom, that fell into the empire under Conrad the Salic, very well defined. The difficulties of government ended, however, as far as eastern Alemannia was concerned, by the erection of Swabia into a distinct duchy. This was created by Henry IV. in favour of his son-in-law, Frederick I. of Hohenstaufen, father of the Emperor Conrad. This line of dukes of Swabia ended in Conradin. About the same time the rest of Alemannia, including Switzerland, was placed under Berthold of Zähringen, whose family, called dukes of Zähringen, became extinct in 1218, having acquired large portion of Burgundy and neighbouring lands. Another part or subdivision was the landgraviate of Alsace, which devolved on Rudolf of Hapsburg in his early days. The margraves of Baden succeeded to a good deal of the possessions of Zähringen, but Frederick II. added more of them to the imperial domain, and they shared the dismemberment of Swabia, whilst some of them fell to the Hapsburgs.

Bavaria.—Bavaria remained in its integrity from the beginning of the empire to the middle of the twelfth century, when the eastern portion of it was attached to the old margraviate of Austria, and a new duchy created for Henry Jochsamergott, uterine brother of Conrad of Franconia, in 1142. It was his line that came to an end in Frederick of Baden. But a further dismemberment took place in 1180, when, in the general subdivision of the estates of Henry the Lion, the county of Tyrol was cut off, and with divers other scattered estates erected into a duchy for the Count of Andsechs, another Berthold, now called Duke of Meraniâ, and best known, probably, as the father of the unfortunate Agnes of Meran, the wife of Philip Augustus. The line of the dukes of Meraniâ became extinct in 1248. Thus,

together with the extinction of the house of Hohenstaufen, coincided the escheating of two very considerable duchies.   But farther east, and never completely
united with either Bavaria or Austria, was Carinthia,
also a duchy, for sometime governed by the descendants
of the ancient kings of Bavaria.   The dukes of Carinthia,
who were also margraves of Verona and Istria, sprang
from the counts of Eppenstein, established there by
Conrad II. in 1027, and these also ended shortly before
the election of Rudolf; Ottocar of Moravia and Bohemia
securing to himself the inheritance.

The forfeiture of Ottocar left then these estates open
to subdivision, and a large portion of the inheritance of
Zähringen and Merania, whose present possessors had
but little right to the tenure, might be reapportioned at
the same time.   Rudolf was in no hurry to do this;
indeed, it was not completed until five years after the
death of Ottocar; two of which years were spent by
the king in travelling up and down Germany making
peace, putting down the robber counts and knights, and
earning the title under which he was hailed by the
Germans with the truly royal title of *Lex Animata.*

Diet at Augsburg, 1282.—At Christmas 1282, at a diet at
Augsburg, he proceeded to divide the escheats.   This he
did with the consent, very grudgingly granted, of the
electors who had served him well against Ottocar.   To
Albert and Rudolf, his two remaining sons, he gave
Austria, Styria, and Carniola; to Meinhard, Count of
Goritz, who had Tyrol, he gave Carinthia, giving the
palatinate of Carinthia to his brother Albert.   Rudolf he
also made Landgrave of Alsace, and, according to some
writers, the duchy of Swabia.   He also confirmed the
landgraviate of Thuringia to the Margrave of Meissen,
and bestowed many smaller fiefs on those whom, having

unauthorised possession, he wished to attach to himself
by the confirmation of their tenure. This settlement of
Germany is well worth observation, as the greatest
readjustment which had taken place for a century.
Amongst other acts he separated the palatinate of
Saxony from the landgraviate of Thuringia, when he
gave the latter to the Margrave of Meissen, bestowing
it on his son-in-law, Duke Albert of Saxony, who thus
reunited the imperial and feudal titles to jurisdiction in
Saxony, which had been divided since 1180.

Rudolf's Relations with England.—The quarrel with
Gregory X., the war with Ottocar, and the redivision
of South Germany are the three most important and
interesting events of the reign of Rudolf. One other
point which is of some interest is—his relations with
England. Edward I. of England, nephew to Richard,
King of the Romans, and brother-in-law to Alfonso
the Wise, his competitor, who also bore the title, was
one of those princes who looked rather shyly at
the adventurer Rudolf, who had undertaken the
task of reconstructing the empire. He calls him in
his early years by no more dignified title than that
of a certain Count of Alemannia. But, before he
had been long on the throne, he thought better of
it, and, even before the final peace of Rudolf with the
pope, negotiations were begun for the marriage of one
of Edward's daughters with Hartmann, Rudolf's son,
who, according to the agreement made, was to inherit
Alsace and the Swiss possessions of his family, and to
have the kingdom of Burgundy revived in his person.
The kingdom of Burgundy, to which Provence and
Arles still nominally belonged, was being rapidly
alienated from the empire by the constant aggressions
of France. Edward had a fellow-feeling that Aquitaine,

which in former years had extended so nearly to the
Burgundian frontier, was rapidly going the same way,
and both monarchs probably considered that the erection of a compact little kingdom would be a greater
contribution to the peace of Europe than the constant
maintenance of a weak hold on the extreme border
provinces of either house. The negotiations hung fire;
Hartmann was to become king of the Romans as soon
as his father became emperor; but constant delays
were interposed, and the whole thing came to an end
by the death of Hartmann, who was drowned in the
Rhine in 1281; but very close relations subsisted
between the two kings, who, as judges and peace-
makers, as well as aggressors, had a good deal in
common, down to the death of Rudolf.

The Close of Rudolf's Reign.—The reign of Rudolf
after the year 1282 contains little besides the pacification
of feuds which had long prevailed, and indeed prevailed
long after his hand was withdrawn. In North Germany
his influence was very slightly felt, notwithstanding his
sincere and laborious efforts to do his duty. Amongst
matters of local importance we can detect one or two
of constitutional significance.

In 1286 he brought the wild Count Eberhard of
Würtemburg to submission, and attempted to secure
order in Swabia by fortifying and confirming the privileges of the imperial cities. In 1287 he issued a document in German, called a recess, published in a diet
at Würzburg, and proclaiming peace for three years.
This is one of the earliest existing public acts in the
German language, and on it probably is founded the
tradition that Rudolf introduced the vernacular language
as the legal language of Germany. The tradition seems
untrue, but it affords another point in which German

and English growth may be compared. In 1290 Rudolf determined the quarrel between the King of Bohemia and the two branches of the Bavarian Government as to the electoral vote. He decided that the dukes of Bavaria and the County Palatine had but one vote between them, and that the seventh vote in the electoral college belonged to Bohemia.

Another set of incidents relates to the old kingdom of Burgundy, which he was anxious to recover for the empire if not for his own family. In this attempt he had little more than legal success. The hand of France was too tight on Provence and Dauphinè; and even the free county of Burgundy, which had been held by Frederick Barbarossa, and since his time by the descendants of his grand-daughter Beatrice, daughter of Otto of Hohenstaufen, was gradually becoming French. In order to augment his influence in that quarter Rudolf married, in his old age, a Burgundian princess of fourteen. But neither fighting nor marrying effected more than the retaining the nominal allegiance of the county during his life. And the same was allowed both in Provence and Dauphinè, whose rulers received investiture at his hands. His own family interest lay in that direction, and neither Philip III. nor Philip IV. was anxious to break with him. Putting aside, then, the Italian transactions, in which Rudolf very wisely intermeddled but slightly, leaving the popes to execute their own policy, the reign of Rudolf contains little that is obscure, although what it does contain cannot be said to be of the highest interest. To the Austrian partisan Rudolf is a hero, almost a demigod. To the Prussian, or extreme Protestant, he is a wretched tool of the papacy, a mere avaricious, unscrupulous adventurer, above all, the founder of the house of Haps-

burg. In reality he seems a fairly good king, anxious
for the safety and wealth of his house as kings are for
the most part, a just man and a peacemaker, and an
especially good manager to maintain friendly relations
with both pope and Germany; but he could not undo
the result of half a century of anarchy. He was disappointed in 1290, in the Frankfort diet, in getting his
son Albert[1] elected as his successor, and died soon
after, July 15, 1291, at Germersheim. He is buried at
Spires with the Franconian kings.

[1] They said the land was too poor to maintain two kings.

IMPORTANT DATES

Rudolf of Hapsburg, 1273–1291.
Wars against Ottocar of Bohemia, 1277–1278.
Diet of Augsburg, 1282.
War with Burgundy, 1288–1289.
League of the Swiss Cantons, 1291.

CHAPTER V

The Succession.—Three short reigns, but not unimportant,
follow the epoch-making one of Rudolf of Hapsburg.
In discussing them we can take up by the way one or
two important questions which they introduce us to;
they are those of Adolf of Nassau, Albert of Austria,
and Henry of Luxemburg. Rudolf, notwithstanding the
strength of the position that he had created for himself
and for his family in South Germany, notwithstanding
the prudent marriages of his daughters and his own wise
and prudent management of the ecclesiastical interest,
had failed to induce the electors to choose his son
Albert as partner or successor to himself in the German
kingdom. In this he paid the penalty of his own caution
in respect to the imperial crown; for, had he ever been
crowned, and a real vacancy occurred in the place of
the King of the Romans, the reluctance of the electors
to appoint one would have been overcome, and then
Rudolf might have been strong enough to secure Albert's
election. But as it was, the ready excuse was that there
was no real vacancy, and the character of Albert for
cruelty and unscrupulousness was so well known that
the princes were glad of any pretext for refusing him.
Rudolf's death left the throne without even an inchoate

claim upon the succession (July 15, 1291). Albert was, of course, the most prominent candidate, but anything like a unanimous election was not to be hoped for. Wenzel IV., King of Bohemia, son of Ottocar (reigns 1278 to 1305), was his rival, and, being himself an elector, had, of course, an initial advantage. If either Albert or Wenzel were chosen the result would have been a war of extermination between Austria and Bohemia, and this the other electors probably felt. After nine months of intrigue, during which Albert was fully persuaded that he should be the winner, the electors met at Frankfort; and, to the astonishment of the world, their choice fell on Adolf, Count of Nassau, a member, as Rudolf had been, of a house which had not yet attained princely rank, but, what was more efficacious, a near relation of Gerard of Eppstein, Archbishop of Mainz, the most able and crafty of the ecclesiastical electors. As the election in this case is said to have been unanimous, it is obvious that it must have been a compromise; according to one account there were four votes against two, and as we know, from documentary evidence, that the Elector of Saxony had promised his vote to Wenzel, it is probable that Adolf was brought forward, on the withdrawal of Albert and Wenzel, in despair of a unanimous election. He was elected May 1, 1292, at Frankfort; and crowned on June 24 at Aix-la-Chapelle.

Accession of Adolf, 1292.—Adolf was a young and gallant prince, but very poor, and hampered, from the very beginning of his reign, with the obligations he had incurred in securing his position. Before he was crowned he had to pledge his castle of Cöbern for 2000 marks to pay the expenses of his election, and to pledge a portion of the imperial domain to Wenzel as a security for the marriage-settlement of his daughter, Guta, who

F

was to marry Rupert, Wenzel's son, and to cement a
family alliance against the Hapsburgs. The choice of
so insignificant a person is a proof of the strong feeling
of the princes against an hereditary dynasty, that curious feeling which we have seen so often unreasonably
displayed at an earlier period, however seldom it succeeded in preventing the odious measure from being
taken; but against which Frederick Barbarossa and
Henry IV. seemed to strive in vain, and for which the
best vindication was the misery that had befallen Germany from the hereditary policy of the Hohenstaufen.
Notwithstanding this, the terms on which Adolf secured
his election were sufficiently stringent, and seem little
else than an actual purchase of the sovereign title; a
purchase more absurd than that of Richard of Cornwall,
who, at least, had the money to pay, and was not forced
to submit to any degrading conditions. Of Adolf it
may be said that his ambition was from the beginning
certain ruin to him; the obligations he entered into with
the ecclesiastical princes, especially the Archbishop of
Mainz, were sufficient to make him their slave; want of
money compelled him to serve as a mercenary in the
wars of Edward of England; want of money compelled
him to acquiesce in the sale of large portion of imperial
Burgundy to France, and want of money placed him
in the position of complete subserviency to the pope.
Much of this was foreseen as early as his coronation,
which took place at Aix-la-Chapelle on Midsummer Day
1292. He lived six years after, and his career was
one distinctly of labour and sorrow. He was, as the
creature of the ecclesiastical electors, immediately
dubbed the *Pfaffenkönig;* and, by way of confirmation
of the popular opinion, may be adduced the fact that,
by his initial bargain with the Archbishop of Mainz, he

gave up or renounced the power of intermeddling with ecclesiastical suits, and confirmed to the archbishop and clergy all their immunities, secular and spiritual; and he further bound himself as surety for Archbishop Gerard to the pope in a sum which he failed to pay, and which rendered him liable at every moment to the papal dictation.

Adolf's Relations with England and France.—Adolf makes hardly any figure in the politics of Europe: such mention of him as there is, is chiefly in connection with the wars of Philip the Fair and Edward I. It would have been his interest to have made an alliance with his nearest neighbour; but as he was without money and without prudence he chose to make France his enemy. Having made a treaty with Edward in 1294 by which he received 30,000 marks for the maintenance of his forces, he was emboldened to throw himself into a French war. Albert of Austria then immediately declared for the French. But, as the war was carried on very slowly both by Edward and Adolf, the year 1297 was reached without much bloodshed.

Adolf spent his money in the purchase of Thuringia, on the possession of which he intended to found a family. As it happened, peace was made between England and France in 1298, before Adolf had had time to strike a blow for his wages, and his fall followed too quickly after this to allow Edward to call him to account. The fact of his having served as a mercenary under Edward of England was made a source of complaint against him by the German princes. In the circumstances in which they were this goes for little, as they were anxious to use any pretext to get rid of him; but it is worth noticing as an instance of the animus of the ancient German people with respect to England, which is throughout much of

their history more easily traced than accounted for;
and which both then and later, down to a comparatively
modern period, was returned with interest from our side.
This feeling of dislike, and even contempt, is traceable
in the German accounts of Richard I., John and Henry
III., and we now see it exemplified in the case of
Edward I. It was very different from the earlier feeling
that subsisted between North Germany and England,
and had shown itself in mutual good offices and many
close alliances. I have sometimes thought that it might
be traced to the connection of the Welfs in Germany
with Henry II. and his sons, and that we had shared the
odium into which, after the triumph of Frederick II.
over Otto, the Welfic party had fallen, the feeling long
surviving the occasion that had called it forth. But I
am not very sure of this, and it would not account for
the corresponding feeling in England. English influence was, however, generally rated at a money value;
and the money of our kings had been poured lavishly
into Germany. With the money paid for the ransom of
Richard I., Henry VI. furnished his Italian expeditions,
and Leopold of Austria built the walls of Vienna; English money had maintained Richard of Cornwall and
his court and laid the foundations of the fortunes of
many a noble house: now English money purchased
Thuringia for Adolf of Nassau, and at the same time
accelerated his disgrace.

Another point, and it is also the practical result of
Adolf's attitude towards France and England, was the
loss of the imperial hold on the old kingdom of Arles,
Burgundy, or Provence, which I mentioned before.
After leading an army as far as Besançon to reclaim
the kingdom, and with it the crown of thorns, the heir-
loom of the royalty of Burgundy, preparatory to taking

any action, Adolf sent a letter of defiance or challenge to Philip the Fair, as Frederick Barbarossa had done to Saladin. Philip, however, was more than a match for poor Adolf, and, although no great battle was fought in the war, the Germans had the worst of it; and the next year Count Otto made over the county of Burgundy, in fact and right, to King Philip for the sum of 100,000 livres, for the marriage of his daughter Jeanne with Philip the Long, son of Philip IV., afterwards Philip V. The Burgundians strongly objected to being sold as sheep, but in vain. Adolf could not help them, and Albert, his successor, could not. The county was separated from the imperial jurisdiction from this time to the reign of Lewis XI., when it became a bone of contention again among the estates of Charles the Bold.

The Purchase of Thuringia.—The only remaining act of importance in Adolf's reign is the purchase of Thuringia, which he bought of Albert the landgrave, who had disinherited his sons out of hatred for their mother. Adolf, attempting to take possession of his ill-gotten bargain, involved himself in a war of four years' duration, in which he obtained no lasting advantage, and gained a sad name as a cruel devastator of the country that he was sworn to protect. In all these transactions he showed no good quality except personal bravery, and this amounted to rashness. The contempt into which he had fallen would, however, have scarcely been enough to secure his deposition had he not been watched by a most able and crafty enemy, Albert of Austria. And thus the end came about.

Election of Albert of Austria, 1297.—At Whitsuntide 1297 Gerard of Mainz, Albert of Austria, and the electors of Saxony and Brandenburg met at Prague at the coronation of King Wenzel, and arranged a conspiracy against the King of the Romans. The execution of this was impeded by the rapid action of Adolf, whose army besieged the archbishop, and prevented him from executing the plan at the moment. Emissaries were sent to Pope Boniface VIII. to persuade him to assent to the deposition of Adolf, and when this failed, for Boniface was faithful to the *Pfaffenkönig*, a second convention was held at Vienna early in 1298. In conformity with an arrangement then made, the princes summoned a diet at Frankfort for May 1, to which both Adolf and Albert, to whom they had already offered the crown, were summoned. This was followed by a court at Mainz on June 23, in which Adolf was deposed and Albert elected. The charges against him were general incapacity and uselessness, the destruction of churches, the corruption of virgins, the serving the King of England for pay, and the cruelties exercised in Thuringia and Meissen. The accusation was made and the sentence pronounced by the electors of Mainz, Saxony, and Brandenburg, both parties claiming, it would seem, the protection and authority of the pope and the consent of the other electors. At the same time they promulgated the election of Albert.

Adolf was not, however, left without promises of support; the Count Palatine and the Archbishop of Trèves were faithful, and the Bavarian dukes, with the imperial cities, united by fear of Albert's aggressions, were at least not hostile to him. But Adolf was in too great a hurry to fight; ten days after the deposition (July 2, 1298) he met his enemy in force at Gellenheim, near Worms, received his first wound, it was said, from Albert himself, and afterwards perished in the *mêlée*. He was ultimately buried at Speyer. I can mention no important constitutional act of his except the confirmation of Rudolf's decision as to the seventh electorate. He was, perhaps, the least regarded and the least important, although not the most insignificant personally, of the whole long line of German kings.

Albert's Re-election, 1298.—Albert of Hapsburg now saw himself at the summit of ambition, for which both he and his father had struggled. There was now no competitor; the influences that had been adverse to him six years before, Gerard (1288 to 1306), the Archbishop of Mainz, and King Wenzel, were partners in his conspiracy and success. No time was lost. The electors met at Frankfort on July 27, 1298, less than a month after the death of Adolf; and Albert, having then renounced the election which had been made at Mainz in June, was re-elected unanimously, and a month after crowned by the Archbishop of Cologne at Aix-la-Chapelle. But the papal recognition was not granted. Boniface VIII. was not likely to confirm the election of one who, in his eyes, was a rebel, a conspirator, and a murderer, and who, moreover, had married a wife connected even remotely with the Hohenstaufen, and half-sister, by the mother, to Conradin. But he went further than refusing confirmation. He excommunicated the king elect; took to himself the title of vicar-general of the empire, and received the ambassadors of Albert, girt with a sword, and crowned with the crown of Constantine. "I am the Emperor" was the answer he returned to them; and he did not cease to urge the electors to proceed to a purer and more regular election, until the year 1303, when, having quarrelled with Philip the Fair, and found himself in need of a powerful friend, he turned round, recognised, absolved, and confirmed his former enemy.

The history of Albert's transactions with Philip and the pope constitutes his contribution to the general politics of Europe; his acts in Austria proper, Hungary, and Bohemia are those which have decided his place in German history; but the fact is that it was his mismanagement of his family and imperial interest among the mountains and lakes of Alemannia, which was the occasion of Swiss independence, and of so much, both in politics and religion, that has resulted from the attitude then taken up by the Forest Cantons, that gives him his place, a very unenviable one, in the history of the world.

These branches of Albert's personal history succeed one another in point of time, and in this way we will look at them.

Albert and Philip the Fair.—I. Albert, as Duke of Austria, had declared himself on the side of France, when King Adolf was serving, or placing himself in condition to serve, as a mercenary of Edward of England. Now Philip the Fair was beginning his political struggle with Boniface VIII., and the opposition, shown and proved by that pope to Albert, had the effect of drawing together these two worthies, the two most unscrupulous persons who ever, I imagine, reigned contemporaneously in Europe. The *rapprochement*, as usual, took the form of a matrimonial alliance; Blanche, the daughter of Philip the Fair, was betrothed to Rudolf, the son of Albert. The fathers met and arranged the match at Vaucouleurs in Lorraine, and, at the same time, determined the limit of their respective countries on the Meuse. The same year Albert quarrelled with the ecclesiastical electors, and withdrew from them their mercantile dues on the Rhine, cutting off thereby a considerable part of their revenues. Rudolf the Count Palatine, as imperial judge, took part with them, and thus reconstituted the old party that had adhered to Adolf; but Albert, adopting the traditional policy of the emperors, marshalled the free towns against them, and compelled submission. He exercised, in fact, the imperial rights more fully than his father had done throughout North Germany, although he was foiled in an attempt to get possession of the county of Holland as an imperial escheat. This year, 1300, witnessed the widening of the quarrel between Philip and Boniface, and, although Albert and the pope were not yet drawn together, Albert and Philip were somewhat drawn asunder. For a part of the new policy of the pope in Italy was the bestowal of Naples on Charles of Valois, brother of Philip, and he did not limit his promises to this; if Charles were able to expel the hated house of Aragon he might look for the imperial crown, now refused to the excommunicated Albert, possibly that of Constantinople also, or at least the titular one, to which his wife, a Courtenay, had some sort of claim. The introduction of Charles into Italy only served, however, to make the pope still more unpopular than before, and it is needless to say that it had no result in Germany. When Philip and Boniface sank all their small quarrels in the great one of 1303, Boniface soon reconciled himself with Albert, and thenceforth they were friends during the few months the pope lived.

Albert and Bohemia.—II. It was in 1302 that the quarrel with Bohemia began in earnest; Albert had of course never forgiven King Wenzel for the share he had taken against him in the election of 1292, or given up the hope of adding both Bohemia and Hungary to his Austrian estates. The line of St.

Stephen of Hungary expired in 1302, in Albert's son-in-law Andrew; and, much as he would have liked to keep Hungary for himself, rather than see it added to Bohemia, as it was likely to be, Albert agreed with the pope to force the Neapolitan Carobert on the people who had offered the crown to King Wenzel and his son of the same name. The league between pope and kaiser was successful; the Wenzels were driven out of Hungary; the father died in 1305 and the son in 1306. Albert attempted to place his eldest son Rudolf on the throne, but he died without issue in 1307; and the rival competitor, Henry of Carinthia, was allowed to succeed to Bohemia on condition of settling the succession on the house of Austria, Hungary being given up to Carobert. The bearing of the episode on Albert's proceedings is chiefly the increase of infamy which he acquired by his cruelty in both Bohemia and Hungary, an infamy which his administration in Austria, from the early days when he acted as his father's heir-tenant, had earned for him, probably with justice. His war with Bohemia was succeeded by one in Thuringia, where he took up the cause of the cities against the landgrave, Frederick with the Bitten Cheek. Happily in this he was beaten, and before he was able to execute his ordinary savage vengeance there he died.

Albert and Switzerland.—III. The war for the emancipation of Switzerland began in 1307. I have mentioned several times already the relations of this territory with the house of Hapsburg: lying between Burgundy and Swabia, the mountain country had, until the extinction of the house of Zähringen, rejoiced in a succession of wise princes who have sought to perpetuate order and to increase civilisation by the foundation of city communities.

On the extinction of the house of Zahringen, and the
subsequent break up of Swabian unity, the mountain
country, like the plain country, broke into divers
communities; the little counts became almost independent rulers; the bishops the same; the imperial cities
cultivated the spirit of independence; and the country
districts, where there were few counts and no cities,
retained the organisation, almost republican and very
free, which they had inherited from the early Teutonic
institutions, and had enjoyed to the full under the
dukes of Zähringen. Rudolf of Hapsburg had made
it one step towards the attainment of his exalted
position, to fight the battles of the imperial towns
against their oppressors; and the country districts
also had hailed him as their *advocatus* or landvogt, a
powerful protector against the aggressions of the neighbouring counts. He himself was Landgrave of Alsace
and Count of Hapsburg; and his grandfather had held
the office of Landvogt of Uri, Schweitz, and Unterwalden.
About 1240 these cantons had shaken off the authority
of the landvogt; but about 1257, in order to secure the
protection of Rudolf, they had voluntarily placed themselves under him. The office of landvogt involved the
fulfilment of the duty of jurisdiction and protection, but
not more: he was an imperial officer answering in some
measure to an English high sheriff, with a tendency, of
course, to become hereditary, and to extend his lawful
powers to unlawful practices. After Rudolf became
King of the Romans, his relations with the cantons
became much less friendly than they had been: his
interests were now imperial rather than local, and the
Swiss began to find that their chosen protector was the
person against whom they most needed protection.
Still Rudolf was generally just, and his administration

popular. Switzerland was to have formed part of Hartmann's kingdom of Burgundy; after Hartmann's death the younger Rudolf, as Duke or Landgrave of Alsace, governed until 1290, when he died, the year before his father, leaving a son John, possessed of a good deal of local influence, whom his uncle Albert at once cheated out of his rights, taking the whole inheritance of King Rudolf to himself.

During the reign of Adolf, Albert, being employed in other schemes, the cantons seem to have been left alone, but only to feel more severely the change when Albert, with the compound claims of his family and royal position, became their sole ruler. He seems to have formed a plan of creating, out of the mountain lands, a new dukedom of Helvetia, to be added to those already held by his house, and proposed to the cantons that they should exchange their immediate relation to the empire —a relation not altered by the mission of the landvogts —for the feudal subjection to a branch of his own family. This they refused; they demanded the renewal of the landvogtship, and Albert granted their request. He sent two landvogts, Herman Gessler and Besenger of Landenberg: these men, by wanton tyranny, provoked the conspiracy of the Forest Cantons in 1307, headed by Walter Fürst, Werner Stauffacher, and Arnold of Melchthal (November 11, 1307).

Albert's Death and Character, 1308.—On the last day of the year the confederates seized the Castle of Rotzberg in Unterwalden. This provoked Albert, as well it might. He himself came into the mountain land to enforce obedience; and there, within sight of his father's castle of Hapsburg, on the plain of Königfelden, as he crossed the river Reuss, his nephew John, whom he had deprived of his inheritance, fell on him and slew him. It was on May 1, 1308; and the act ranks among the most signal crimes of European history, rather perhaps from its circumstances, the relation of the murderer to his victim, the mature age of Albert, who was about sixty, contrasted with the youthful violence of his nephew, and the fact that the scene lay within sight of the cradle of his family, the house in which probably he was born and bred.

Albert's character requires no summing up; he was wise, *i.e.* politic and brave; but very ambitious, unjust, and cruel. The strength of his character was spent on the aggrandisement of his house rather than on realising the influence or doing the duties of his position as the chosen leader of the German people and the elect head of the empire. He is the seventh king of Germany, elected since Frederick II., who has made no real claim to the imperial crown; and the sixth who had not set foot in Italy as kings or emperors. He scarcely even made a pretence to Italian interest. He left several sons, whose history belongs to the next and following reigns; and five daughters, the best known of whom is Agnes, widow of Andrew of Hungary, who avenged her father's death in a spirit akin to his own.

The vigour of Albert had a bracing effect on the German kingdom. Selfish as his own policy was, the people felt that they had a man, and not a mere shadow, at their head; and, although he led them to no great enterprise, he in a way prepared them for the dawn of a better day, short though the better day was. Such was the next reign, that of Henry of Luxemburg, in whom the German kingdom again asserts its right to the imperial dignity.

The election of a successor to Albert promised to be a stormy one. The King of France, in whose hands the pope, Clement V., now resident at Avignon, was naturally supposed to be, was known to covet the imperial crown for himself, and if that were not feasible, for his brother Charles of Valois; and the young dukes of Austria were also anxious to put forth their claims, expecting no doubt a refusal, but thinking that by claiming the greater dignity they might secure the smaller one, and, if they missed the empire, might be safe to get investiture of their father's estates.

Election of Henry VII., 1308.—But happily the election was decided neither by the bullying of Philip the Fair nor by appeal *ad misericordiam* of the desolate young Hapsburgs. It was decided by the genius of Peter, Archbishop of Mainz, who had looked round him for a man of honesty, valour, and discretion, and had found him in Henry, Count of Luxemburg, a small potentate on the borders of Lorraine, but a brave and good prince. It is too long to tell how it all came about, but it was in a few words thus :—the majority of the lay electors, Saxony, Brandenburg, and the Palatine, held a caucus before the election, and determined to vote for the one of six on whom the clerical electors should decide; the six were the two Margraves of Brandenburg, the two Counts Palatine, Albert of Hanau, and Frederick of Austria. Peter of Mainz, on the other hand, had proposed, to Baldwin of Trèves, the choice of Henry of Luxemburg, who was Baldwin's brother, and then persuaded the lay electors to extend their agreement, and choose the ecclesiastical candidate : this was done. Henry of Luxemburg was chosen on November 27, 1308, and crowned at Aix-la-Chapelle on January 6, 1309.

Henry was the representative of the same class of nobles from which William of Holland had sprung;

was descended in the female line from that Sigefred
of Luxemburg, whose daughter, Cunigunda, was wife
of Henry II., the Saint; and had, in his early years,
fought against Edward I. of England in the army of
Philip the Fair. He was one of the princes present at
the coronation in 1308 of Queen Isabella and Edward
II. He was the most accomplished knight of his time,
and his career proved him to be worthier of the title
that he had won than any claimant since Frederick II.
His incipient difficulties were easily arranged: Clement
V., who had been acting quietly and surely in contravention of the design of his master, King Philip, hardly
pretended reluctance when asked to confirm the election. The allegiance of the Austrian dukes was secured
by the grant of investiture which Henry promised even
before his coronation; and from the princes who had
chosen him, and who apparently thought they had little
to fear from so poor and small a prince, he in turn had
nothing to apprehend.

His First Acts.—His first act, however, showed his
spirit; he sent forthwith to the pope to demand the
imperial crown, and, like a brisk suitor, insisted on
his naming the day. Clement was chafing under the
yoke of Philip, and threw himself cordially, although
quietly, into the German alliance: he fixed the day,
February 2, two years. One of Henry's next acts
was to nominate a landvogt for the Forest Cantons,
and to confirm other privileges. From the beginning of his reign it was clear that his face was set
towards Italy. He was not, as we shall see, careless
about the interests of his family, or of the great duty
exemplified by Rudolf of Hapsburg, of increasing his
hereditary influence, but he was throughout an emperor
on the model of the Ottos, of Henry III., and Frederick

Barbarossa, although with the pope instead of against him; he was the ideal monarch of Dante's Monarchia, under whom righteousness and peace were to be restored to Italy. In August 1309, at Spires, where he was holding a diet, for the purpose, among others, of burying his two predecessors in the imperial chapel, he announced his intention of marching into Italy. In the same diet, as if preparatory, he reinvested the Austrian dukes; resigned his hereditary estates to his son John, and raised the county of Luxemburg to a duchy; and received the runaway heiress of Bohemia, the daughter of the elder Wenzel, who came to offer her hand in marriage to his son John, the new-made duke. Henry, after some hesitation, it is said, accepted the proposal. John became thereupon King of Bohemia, and territorially laid the foundation of the imperial house of Luxemburg, which, after nearly a century and a half of empire, blended with Austria, in the marriage of Albert II. with Elizabeth, the daughter of Sigismund. Henry of Carinthia, the intrusive King of Bohemia, was overthrown, and the triumphant Archbishop Peter—triumphant, I mean, in his grand scheme founded on the election of Henry—crowned John of Luxemburg king. This is that John of Bohemia who, blind and poor, having seen his son Charles elected emperor, fell at the battle of Crecy, and whose cognisance is borne still by the Prince of Wales. A year intervened between the diet of Spires and the beginning of the Italian expedition, a year spent in reconciling quarrels and providing for the defence of the kingdom during his absence.

The Templars.—It was during this year that the persecution of the Templars was being carried on in France and Italy. In Germany, however, that unfortunate body

of men, whose condemnation by pope and king is one
of the greatest crimes and abominations of the Middle
Ages, was comparatively free from harm.   The lying
accusations were brought against them there as elsewhere; but, bad as the times were, the honest and true
German spirit was too strong to yield to Philip the Fair.
The Templars were acquitted.   The order, however, was
dissolved by a papal decree, and its estates divided.   The
Teutonic order in Germany, as the Hospitallers, both
there and in other countries, came in probably for what
little, after royal and papal charges, was left—the impoverished estates and ruined preceptories.

Expedition to Italy, and Death, 1313.—In October
1310, Henry marched from Lausanne into Piedmont.
In close alliance with Clement V.—a Guelf king
and a Ghibelline pope; the king, a few years before
the mercenary, and the pope still the prisoner, almost,
of the French king against whose kinsman Robert of
Naples, and French influence in Italy, the expedition
was virtually projected.   The Guelfs and the Ghibellines
alike were perplexed with the combination; sometimes
one, sometimes the other yielded; sometimes one, and
sometimes the other resisted.   On the whole, until he
reached Milan, Henry's march was triumphant.   On
January 6, 1311, he received the iron crown of
Lombardy at Milan, and all Lombardy, except Verona,
recognised his title.   But then and there the tide began
to turn.   Milan, urged to revolt by the Guelfic faction,
broke into insurrection, provoked, it is said, by the
measures taken by Henry to secure the city whilst he
marched southwards.   The example was followed by
other towns, especially Brescia.   For four months
Henry was kept before Brescia.   In this time the
freshness and hopefulness of the expedition faded
away. Still, in November, Henry got on to Genoa,

G

where his queen died.   He had already lost his brother
Waleram in the siege of Brescia.   At Genoa he had
tidings from Naples.   King Robert proposed a marriage,
but before any conclusion was come to, Henry heard that
John of Achaia, Prince of the Morea, Robert's brother,
had entered Rome with an armed force in concert with
the Guelfic Orsini.   In March he advanced to Pisa, the
Ghibelline city.   From Pisa he went on to Rome.   But,
although he arrived there with the cardinals commis-
sioned to crown him, the Guelfic party, who had long
sunk political principles in family feuds and personal
hatreds, the Orsini against the Colonnas, backed up by
that baneful French influence from Naples, which had
been the curse of Italy, a much worse curse than German
interference, for fifty years, refused to welcome him, and
held the Church of St. Peter against him.   Henry was,
as Otto had been, too weak in forces to occupy by force
the whole of Rome : he was crowned at the Lateran on
the feast of the Apostles, June 29, 1312.   The fatal gift
brought its usual luck to the Germans.   The resistance
of the Guelfs at Rome encouraged them to revolt elsewhere.   Florence started a new league; Pisa was the
headquarters of the emperor.   A year of unavailing war
ensued.   The best energies of the best German king
were wasted in Tuscany; and in August 1313 he died,
poisoned, as it was believed, by a priest in the very cup
of the Eucharist.

His Character.—To see the result of this terrible end
in Italy, Milman's chapter on the Italian war and on
the Monarchia of Dante should be read.   The delays
and disasters in Italy had been too effectual in
Germany.   Henry of Carinthia had rebelled and tried
to unseat the young King of Bohemia, and Baldwin of
Trèves, the emperor's brother, had found himself prevented by that war from sending a due proportion of

succour to Italy. Perhaps Henry's death saved him from greater and more cruel disappointment. The pope even was compelled by Philip to forbid any attack being made on the Neapolitan kingdom; and had his life been prolonged, either it must have been wasted, or a war with France, for which Germany was by no means prepared, must have followed. As soon as he was removed his friends laid the blame of all the mischief upon him; the pope, his friend Clement, turned round and called him a perjurer. But the love and regret of the German people followed him, and the lamentations of all good and wise men prove, more than any actual record of his deeds, how much he was valued, and how great and good a prince his contemporaries thought him. After him, Germany had many brave and good and wise princes, but none who bore such a memory for valour and wisdom and goodness as he did: not one whose history recalls all that is noble and real in chivalry; the glory of the good, rude heroic days of the early kings. We pass, as it were, out of the light and truth of the thirteenth century, that wonderful, if troublous, seedtime of principles and realities, into the gorgeous, chivalrous, unreal, selfish, oppressive, and unprincipled fourteenth: in Henry of Luxemburg, the list of the great sovereigns amongst whom were Edward I. and Lewis IX. ends.

IMPORTANT DATES

Adolf of Nassau, 1292–1298.
Allies with Edward I., 1294.
At war in Flanders against France, 1295.
Albert of Hapsburg, 1298–1308.
Reconciliation with Boniface VIII., 1302.
Presses his claims on Switzerland, 1304.
Henry VII., 1308–1313.
Expedition to Italy, 1310.

CHAPTER VI

Disputed succession in the Empire—Frederick of Austria—Lewis of Bavaria—John XXII's intervention—Success of Lewis—Expedition to Italy—Death of John XXII, 1334—Germany and the Hundred Years' War—Crecy—Condition of Germany—The growing independence of Switzerland—Death of Lewis, 1347.

THE three reigns which have been now considered occupy altogether only twenty-one years; the reign that follows, that of Lewis of Bavaria, embraces thirty-two : it is full of incident, of matter that touches European history generally, and is of great importance, both politically and ecclesiastically.

Election of Lewis IV. and Frederick of Austria.— The death of Henry VII. occurred in August 1313 in Tuscany. The news took Germany very much by surprise; there was, before an election could be made, unfortunately too much time for intrigue. After fourteen months the electors met at Frankfort. On this occasion there was no question as to the place of the seven electors, but, unfortunately, two of the electoral seats were themselves contested. The electorate of Saxony was in debate between the Dukes of Wittenberg and Lauenburg;[1] and there were two strong princes both claiming to be kings of Bohemia, John of Luxemburg and Henry of Carinthia. The two candidates brought

---

[1] Rudolf I. (of the Ballenstadt house, extinct in 1423), son of Albert II, died at Wittenberg, and Palatine as well as Elector; succeeds before 1308, and continues the electoral line. His competitor was John II. of Saxe-Lauenburg (1285 to 1315), son of John I., brother of Albert II. of Saxony and Wittenberg. Lauenburg line extinct in 1689, when the Ascanian house expired.

forward were Lewis, Duke of Bavaria, and Frederick, Duke of Austria, the son of Albert of Hapsburg. John of Bohemia would gladly have succeeded his father, but he was still very young; and he, with his uncle, Baldwin of Trèves, and Peter of Mainz, whose management had secured the election of Henry VII., with the Margrave of Brandenburg, whose representative voted for Lewis contrary to his master's directions, and the Duke of Lauenburg, supported Lewis of Bavaria; the Archbishop of Cologne, the Elector Palatine, Lewis's own brother, Rudolf, the Duke of Wittenberg, and Henry of Carinthia, supported Frederick. There were thus on one side three, and on the other two good and on each side two disputed votes. Frederick's electors got the start of a single day in making election. Each side ignored the disputed votes of the other. Lewis claimed a majority of three votes over Frederick; Frederick claimed a majority of one over Lewis. Both were equally obstinate. Both were proclaimed as elect. Both were crowned on the same day—Lewis at Aix-la-Chapelle, by the Archbishop of Mainz; Frederick at Bonn, by the Archbishop of Cologne: Lewis in the right place, but by the wrong bishop; Frederick by the right bishop, but in the wrong place. Both prepared for war, and each took measures for certifying his election to the pope who was to be; for the papacy itself was vacant by the death of Clement V. in April 1314, nor was John XXII. elected before August 1316.

There was thus no official umpire, had either king or electors been willing to refer the matter to arbitration. Both sides prepared for war, and for eight years a civil war devastated Germany, the pope looking on and congratulating himself, both as a creature of France and as Bishop of Rome, that the two parties in Germany were perhaps preparing the way by suicidal quarrels for a French emperor, but certainly were disabling one another for an attempt to recover the Italian rights of the empire, to interfere with the Guelfic party in the north or with the French-Neapolitan interest in South Italy. The two competitors were old friends, who had unhappily quarrelled over some disputed rights in Bavaria and, having been reconciled, had never entirely returned to their old intimacy. But both were honest and religious men; both were greatly beloved by their own subjects, and both had right enough on their side to make resistance justifiable. Frederick's noble and disinterested character would, however, have led him to peace early in the strife, but for the high spirit and pertinacity of his brother Leopold, who commanded his armies, and sustained his party by intrigue as well as by military skill.

The war between these two princes was very much a war of persons and dynasties, and by no means as yet a war of principles; the pope gave open support to neither of them; as for France, the kings were equally likely to favour the Austrian and the Luxemburg parties, and the Luxemburg party was now on the side of Lewis. John XXII. busied himself with Italy until the Germans should settle their quarrels, and then, no doubt, his policy would be to crush the triumphant claimant, or to make such terms with him as would secure French and Guelfic domination in Italy.

Lewis Triumphant, 1322.—This war continued, then, for eight years (1314 to 1322); then Lewis defeated and took prisoner Frederick at Muhldorf, September 28, 1322, and announced to the pope that he was the sole claimant of the empire. John replied by recommending him to treat his prisoner well, and offering to settle the matter between them. From this moment there was irreconcilable enmity between the pope and Lewis, aggravated by the intrigues of the successive kings of France :—an enmity which ran through three pontificates, and ended in the death of Lewis under sentence of excommunication.

In brief, the friendship between pope and kaiser ended with the death of Henry VII.; and the intolerant, violent, and unscrupulous spirit of John XXII., entering with all the zeal of a Frenchman and a Neapolitan favourite into the designs of France and Naples, was determined to be satisfied with nothing less than the destruction of the imperial power. The relations between him and Lewis may be compared with those of Hildebrand and Henry IV., or with those of Innocent IV. and Frederick II.; but in both the former cases there was something like a true principle on the pope's side, something, at least, beyond the blind hatred of a narrow-minded partisan.

If Lewis of Bavaria is a lower type of character than Henry or Frederick, his antagonist is in an infinitely lower relation to Gregory and Innocent; and the humiliation of Lewis is infinitely more humiliating in many ways than that of his predecessors. They were, at the best, ungodly, irreligious men, trampled on by men whose pride and arrogance rested on a faith in their spiritual rights; but Lewis was obliged to sue in vain for mercy to a pope who was actuated by nothing better than French hatred, and the very piety and humility of the religious king laid him open to more unblushing, more shameless outrage from the spiritual tyrant. No language ever applied, even mistakenly applied, to what is called priestcraft—that is, the use of spiritual influence

to the attainment of merely secular or immoral ends—
is undeserved when applied to John XXII.; he appears
to be a very incarnation of priestcraft.

Lewis and the Papacy.—The battle of Mühldorf indi-
cated at once to the pope which of the two competitors
he was to crush. The first word comes from the pope:
the first act, however, comes from Lewis. Having settled
Germany, he began to look towards Italy. Within a
few months of the battle of Mühldorf, he was enabled,
by the lapse of the margraviate of Brandenburg, to
strengthen his family interest by bestowing it on his
eldest son Lewis. He had been obliged, some years
before, to expel his brother Rudolf from the palatinate,
which he now ruled by his influence over his nephew.
Saxony was friendly, and the war was only kept up
spasmodically by Leopold of Austria, who saw himself
without allies. Lewis might be excused for attempting
to anticipate any move in Italy in favour either of a
new election or of the imprisoned Frederick, or of the
placing Robert of Naples, as he wished to be placed,
on the Italian throne.

Lewis, then, in June 1323, by his General Berthold
drove the Guelfs and Neapolitans out of Milan, and
this opened the breach. But the pope and King
Charles of France were beforehand with him. A month
before, King John of Bohemia was persuaded to marry
his sister Mary to Charles the Fair, the King of France,
and thus became detached from the Bavarian party to
which he had by his own influence and that of his
family been a tower of strength.

On October 8, 1323, Pope John proceeded to summon
Lewis to Avignon to account for his presumption in
calling himself King of the Romans before he had
received papal confirmation, and as such giving away

Brandenburg before the pope had settled the question. He was to appear in two months under penalty of excommunication. The two months elapsed. Lewis protested in vain. After another delay, the pope issued the sentence of excommunication, March 23, 1324. Lewis even then would have done everything for a reconciliation, but no offers would satisfy the pope; the sentence was published.

Struggle with the Papacy.—Lewis of Bavaria was no more to be called King of the Romans. The sentence, as we have seen on former occasions, although sure in its final operation, was slow to work at first. It found, when it reached Germany, the nation boiling over with indignation at the league between France and Bohemia. The whole ecclesiastical party was now ardent in support of the German king. But the French were very confident. Charles the Fair (1322 to 1328) was to be elected king, and the pope would be only too glad to crown him. John of Bohemia would bring all the Luxemburg and Austrian interest to bear on the electors; they would make their election, and Charles was to meet them to receive the crown at Bar-sur-Aube on July 27. Charles was there, but the imperial crown was not; nor one of the electors to apologise: only poor Leopold of Austria, ready to promise heaven and earth to secure the release of his brother. King John had already flown; the poor queen, Mary, whose influence alone held her erratic brother to his bargain, had died in February (1324), and the sudden friendship was coming quickly to an end.

King John, who had an irresistible fondness for attending weddings, attended King Lewis's marriage to Margaret, daughter of William of Holland and sister of Queen Philippa of England, the same month, at Cologne.

The Franciscan party, or the spiritualist faction among them, who regarded the pope as heretical, threw themselves with the most ardent zeal on Lewis's side. The archbishop-electors would not move in obedience to the pope's injunctions. Charles and Leopold alone constituted the papal party; yet again (July 11, 1324) John XXII. summoned Lewis, now the fourth time, to appear at Avignon, and excommunicated his supporters. For a moment it seemed that Lewis was to be victorious, but the French gold and the papal excommunication were working their way. The good Archbishop of Mainz was dead, and a papal nominee was in his place. Baldwin of Trèves, true to the interests of his house, followed the vagaries of John of Bohemia, and the Archbishop of Cologne had always been hostile.

In January 1325, they were almost ready to elect King Charles; but they were checked by a new move of Lewis: he released (March 13, 1325) his rival, Frederick of Austria, renewed his old friendship with him, and received from him a renunciation of his rights as elected King of the Romans and a recognition of his own.

In this story we get again what is rare in German history—a dash of romance. John XXII. and Leopold urged Frederick to break his agreement; but he held true. Finding himself unable to observe all the conditions, he returned to captivity and, having with Lewis set aside the old treaty, made a new secret one by which they were to be joint kings and emperors (September 5, 1325, at Munich), each taking a part in every act of sovereignty; they were to rule on alternate days, or one in Germany and the other in Italy. But the plan got wind; the electors complained that it infringed their rights; the Austrian party applied to the pope to recognise Frederick's claim and to ignore the excommunicated Lewis. But John XXII. dared not propose any emperor but his own King Charles; and, what was more conclusive, Duke Leopold of Austria died early in 1326 (February 28). Frederick refused to be made a tool of any party, and retired altogether into his own estates, where he also died four years after. Lewis at last was without a competitor, and he was ready now to attack Italy in earnest.

Lewis's Italian expedition, justifiable as it was on many grounds of right and precedent, and provoked by the constant unmeaning pertinacious hostility of John XXII., was not popular in Germany. The ecclesiastical princes were ready to plead his excommunication as an excuse for not obeying any distasteful summons, and the secular ones, although bound to appear at Rome at his coronation, were not equally bound to go with him to assert and vindicate his claim.

The year that followed the pacification of Germany was spent rather in arranging the affairs at home than in preparing an army. Lewis would have been unwise to withdraw his own forces from his hereditary estates, nor is there much evidence to show that he possessed such force to any extent. In January 1327 he made his appearance at Trent with 100 knights and two or three great scholars, Ockham, Marsilius of Padua, and John de Janduno. The former were to be the nucleus of the force that the Ghibellines were to provide him, and the latter were to pronounce the pope a pretender and a heretic, which they did before leaving Trent.

The Triumph of Lewis in Italy, 1328.—We cannot but compare this opening of the struggle with that in which Frederick II. began his; a war of books preceded the war of blows, first *verba*, then *verbera*. So he started for Italy; to use the concise and expressive words of Dean Milman, which are indeed a history in epitome of all the German expeditions to Italy :—"So set forth another German emperor, unwarned, apparently ignorant of all former history, to run the same course as his predecessors, a triumphant passage through Italy, a jubilant reception in Rome, a splendid coronation, the creation of an antipope ; then dissatisfaction, treachery, revolt among his partisans, soon weary of the exactions wrung from them, but which were necessary to maintain the idle pageant ; his German troops wasting away with their own excesses and the uncongenial climate, and cut off by war and fever ; an ignominious retreat quickening into flight, the wonder of mankind sinking at once into contempt, the mockery and scoffing joy of his inexorable foes."

From Trent Lewis advanced by Bergamo and Como to Milan. At Como he heard that a revolution in his favour had broken out at Rome. At Milan at Whitsuntide he received the iron crown ; but only excommunicated bishops could be found to crown him. There also by deposing the tyrant, Galeazzo Visconti, who, although a Ghibelline, had made himself intolerable to the Ghibellines as well as the Guelfs, he bought a moment's popularity rather too dearly. At this very juncture he was for the fifth time excommunicated and deprived so far as the papal word could do it of his own hereditary estates and everything else. Lewis advanced slowly towards Rome ; the latter half of the year was spent in Tuscany ; in January he reached the Eternal City, and was crowned emperor at St. Peter's. This was on January 17, 1328. On April 18 he deposed the pope, and on May 13, Ascension Day, created a new one, Peter of Corvara, a Franciscan of the party most opposed to John XXII., on the doctrine of poverty, and an Italian.

This is the zenith of Lewis's fortunes. In September he returned into Tuscany, the usual difficulties to a further march being insuperable ; and Robert of Naples having taken the initiative against the emperor both by land and sea. A series of Guelf revolutions in Lombardy set in at the same time, and Lewis saw some of his most valued allies deposed from their ill won and worse used authority. The Ghibelline cities would not bear the antipope. Inch by inch Lewis disputed the ground, not so much against men as against circumstances ; a year and a half of little mishaps and unvaried failure wearied him, and in December 1329 he was again at Trent, determined to make no more fight for Italy, but, if possible, to reconcile himself with the pope and do what he could in Germany. Lewis quitted Italy in December 1329. Frederick of Austria died January 13, 1330.

The General Situation.—Frederick of Austria was dead. The question was, What would the pope do next ? Some other changes had, in the meantime, taken place in Europe, which were destined in a few years to withdraw the interest of history from Italy to another field. Charles the Fair died in January 1328, and Edward III. of England, who had married a sister-in-law of the emperor, was preparing to claim the succession to the French throne against Philip of Valois. England, instead of being a cipher in European politics, as it had been under Edward II., was about to take a leading part. The league of pope and French king would be weakened by the loss of English money ; and the party of Lewis might look for ready support, at least against France, and probably against a French pope, from the husband of Philippa of Hainault. Had not Lewis of Bavaria been reduced

by his Italian discomfiture to an almost fatal despon-
dency, he might have found comfort in the changed
relations between the pope and the King of France;
for Philip of Valois was much more inclined to act as the
master of John XXII. than as his servant, and his faith
even in the spiritual authority of the old man was
shaken by the accusations of heresy which were poured
out against him unremittingly, both by the stricter
Franciscans on the subject of poverty, and by the
Dominicans on the subject of the state of the saints
in glory and the beatific vision.   But the indomitable
pope was ready to fight with all the world: he would
hear no apology from Lewis; and, if he could not
manage Philip, he would act irrespective of him. Now
again the irrepressible John of Bohemia comes forward
to complicate matters; he makes an expedition to Italy
to arbitrate; his expedition, as was likely, only em-
broils matters the more; the pope is suspected, by the
French, of conniving at it. Two or three years of waiting and comparative rest followed. Lewis used these
to humiliate himself before the pope more than ever;
but it was all in vain. He was only prevented from
resigning the crown by the resolute protest of the
electoral body.

The Hundred Years' War opens, 1337.—In 1334
John XXII. died, and his successor, Benedict XI.,
who would gladly have adopted the policy of Clement
V., found himself tied hand and foot by the French
party, and unable even to relax the sentence of excommunication against Lewis. Two or three more
years passed in humiliating, unavailing negotiations.
In 1337 the war between England and France began;
and with it the hopes of Lewis began again to rise. I
think that, however low the estimate taken by historians

of the power and ability of Lewis of Bavaria may be, we ought to consider in his favour, how firm the hold seems to have been that he had upon Germany during the whole of this struggle. It was not, indeed, much active or energetic support that he got; but note the impossibility, after the death of Frederick of Austria, of setting up an anti-Cæsar against him, defeated, deposed, excommunicated as he was, and robbed by the excommunication of any chance of stirring up a zealous support for him among foreign princes.

In Germany, from the beginning of the wars of Edward III., he might have begun still further to rise in personal influence if his spirit had been equal to his opportunity. The constant refusal of the popes, or rather of the papal court under French influence, to recognise the title of Lewis, provoked beyond endurance what national pride and spirit there was in the German princes; and even the bishops who had been forced by John XXII. on the churches, began to take part in the national feeling. In 1338 diet after diet was held: the electors met at Rhense (July 6) and protested against the pope's position; the pope himself in secret complained that it was by the threats of Philip of Valois that he was compelled to act as he did. The whole German nation repudiated the doctrine that their king required confirmation from an Italian or French bishop, even of Rome.

Lewis and Edward III., 1338.—In September of the same year Lewis and Edward III. concluded their alliance; and Edward was made vicar of the empire in the provinces west of the Rhine; the league was strengthened by communion at mass and the most binding oaths. The connection unfortunately brought neither strength nor credit to either party. Edward was yet far from an experienced warrior, and a wise and faithful man he never became; the opening of the great French war is one of the passages of our history least creditable to our national prudence or common sense. Lewis was too irresolute, or rather too broken-spirited, to press a decided policy; the initial advantages of the struggle were all on the side of Philip. As Philip allowed the pope to hold out promises of absolution to Lewis, he drew off from England. Year after year was wasted in mere negotiation and humiliating bargaining, and at last, in 1342, the death of Pope Benedict put an end to all hope. Clement VI. (1342 to 1352), who succeeded him, was ready to act in the spirit and power of John XXII. He found new grounds of accusation against Lewis; and unfortunately these grounds were common to him and King John of Bohemia. For Lewis, on the death (in 1335) of Henry of Carinthia, Count of Tyrol and ex-King of Bohemia, whose claims on the latter country had been one cause that attached John to the emperor, redistributed the estates of the duke, and a few years later had, by his imperial authority, dissolved the marriage of the heiress Margaret with the son of John of Bohemia, and married her to his son Lewis of Branden-burg. He had previously divided her inheritance, giving Carinthia to the dukes of Austria, John's hereditary enemies, and after the marriage adding the Tyrol, that land most coveted of all and always by Bavaria, to the power and weight if not to the actual territory of his own house. By the marriage of the heiress Lewis incurred the enmity of John, and by the act of annulling the marriage he infringed the spiritual authority of the pope.

The Deposition, 1346, and Death of Lewis, 1347.— In April 1343 Clement VI. excommunicated Lewis

again, and ordered the archbishops to elect a new
king. There was no depth of humiliation which Lewis
would not consent to, if he might be absolved. He
undertook to renounce his dignity, his imperial crown,
his friends, his freedom of action as regarded France,
Bohemia, and Italy; but not even this sufficed. Clement
insisted that he should allow the invalidity of all his acts,
and pray to have them confirmed at Avignon, and that
he should promise to act no more without special per-
mission from the pope. He submitted to all. Then the
Germans took affront, and protested; the pope regarded
this as an infringement of the conditions, and not only
refused the absolution still, but deposed the Archbishop
of Mainz (April 7, 1346), and issued a new bull of excommunication, more terrible, cruel, and blasphemous than
any that had preceded it. This seems to have decided
the struggle. The princes held out no longer against
the order to make a new election. In July 1346 (July
11), at Rhense they met, with the exception of Brandenburg, and elected Charles of Moravia, the eldest son of
John of Bohemia; but he could not get access either to
Frankfort, for the formal election, or to Aix-la-Chapelle,
to be crowned.

A rapid succession of events, as rapid as that of the
preceding years had been slow and wearisome, prevented a general war. Edward III. landed in Nor-
mandy; John of Bohemia and Charles the elect of
Rhense hastened to meet him in arms on the French
side (August 26, 1346), and on the field of Creçy John
closed his troubled and most troublesome career.
Charles succeeded his father as King of Bohemia, and
flying from Creçy to secure his rights, was crowned
King of the Romans at Bonn on November 26.

The defeat of Creçy for the moment checked the

H

policy of Philip and Clement. Germany had time to breathe, and Germany declined to acquiesce in the deposition of Lewis. Charles was, as we shall see, great neither in war nor in policy. Some little advantages he gained, but the bulk of the kingdom stood aloof. Lewis was growing old for an emperor; he was at least sixty (born in 1286), and had had very little rest and very great miseries. He was hunting bears near Munich on October 11, 1347, when he was taken in a fit, and died as he had lived, unabsolved by any earthly power beyond his own innocence and penitence, for crimes that he had not committed.

Character of his Reign.—It has already been re-marked that, whereas the thirteenth century was for Germany the age of disruption and dismemberment, the fourteenth began a period of accretion, which led to the accumulation of great inheritances and the foundation of great families. The reign of Lewis of Bavaria illustrates this. We have seen in Rudolf of Hapsburg the fortune of a Swiss count waxing to the dignity of King of the Romans and founder of the house of Austria; in the case of Henry of Luxemburg, one stroke of good luck creating, out of a petty county of Lorraine, the royal house of Bohemia, with Moravia as a margraviate attached, and large claims on Hungary, Carinthia, and the Tyrol. Fortune was not less kind to Lewis of Bavaria, although he was not destined to found a dynasty.

It will be remembered that in 1322 he was enabled to bestow on one son, Lewis, his eldest son by his first wife, the margraviate of Brandenburg, on the death of his nephew Henry, the last of the Ascanian margraves; and how, in 1341, by an extraordinary exertion of imperial power, he divorced the heiress of Carinthia and Tyrol from her husband, and bestowed her on another. In 1340 the duchy of Lower Bavaria, held by his cousin John, representing the line of Henry of Lower Bavaria, son of Otto, Lewis's grandfather, became extinct, and in spite of the claims of the Counts Palatine, his nephews, Lewis was accepted by the states as sole duke; and in 1345, two years before his death, the death of his brother-in-law, William, Count of Holland, placed him in possession of the great counties of Holland and Hainault, which he bestowed on his wife Margaret, the sister of the late count, and administered by another son, William, who founded the Bavarian line in Holland.

The German Rule of Partition.—By the possession of Holland, Brandenburg, Tyrol, Bavaria, and the Palatinate, the house of Wittelsbach reached the maximum extent of territory that it has ever possessed. But, unfortunately for the purpose of dynastic aggrandisement, the ancient German rule of partition among the sons of the house, split up the domain after every accumulation.

To this rule I must now call your attention in other cases besides Bavaria; for it supplied a corrective in some measure of the accumulative process that was going on. Nothing shows more completely than this how the tenure of power in Germany had changed, since the days of the strong emperors and strong dukes. The idea that an elector, or margrave, or duke owed his authority to the imperial deputation was only recognised when he applied for investiture. So long as that was a reality, it was not the interest either of emperor or vassal to break up the princely possessions of a father amongst his sons. The father knew that his strength depended on keeping together what he had; and the emperor also thought it best that his vassals should have, so to speak, all their eggs in one basket, where, if it were necessary, one blow would dispose of all.

But from the period of the disruption of the empire the idea of founding great houses seems to have taken the place of that of retaining personal power; the latter had given its owner a great advantage whilst the empire was a reality, whilst the sovereign ruled by his diet, and the strongest man in the diet was almost a match for the sovereign. But when this was lost, and every man did what was right in his own eyes, and looked on his estates as his own property, not the gift of a superior or benefice of a vassal, the strength of the house, to be extended by marriages and purchases, but not necessarily to be wielded by one person, became the leading idea; and the old German law, which in England we know as gavelkind, was, it would seem, not yet extinct in spirit. So several of the great houses split up their estates among two or more branches, obtaining from the emperors, who also saw their advantage, a sort of new creation, or, as it is called, *majoratus*, for each branch. These branches strengthened their original connection in many cases by an agreement of *Erbverbrüderung*, or, as we say in English law, cross remainders, by which it was mutually settled that the one should inherit the estates of the other in case of extinction or direct posterity.

Its Results. — The emperors were obliged to yield in many instances to this arrangement, although it defeated their just claims to escheat, especially when, as it often was, the arrangement was made between princes who were not of a common stock. In this way the Saxon princes entirely broke up the union of their house and deprived it of any political weight in Germany. The two branches disputed the electorate between them, and when that question was settled, the electoral house of Wittenberg dwindled away, whilst that of Lauenburg, although much longer lived, lost its right of succession and became quite insignificant. This rule held in this family long after the Reformation, and the present duchies of Saxe-Weimar, Saxe-Meiningen, Saxe-Coburg and Gotha, and Saxe-Altenburg, with the kingdom of Saxony founded on the fragment to which the electorate became attached, survive at the present day to exemplify it. The same rule held in Brunswick and Brandenburg, but in neither of those families was it carried to so great an extent as in Saxony, and other states were more frequently reunited.

Not to pursue it into the smaller duchies, I may mention the case of Bavaria and the Palatinate. The former, after the union of the estates under Lewis, was not subdivided ; but the Palatinate was, and the divisions branched out and succeeded one another as each became extinct, until, at the latter end of the last century, the Elector Palatine succeeded to Bavaria also, from which his family had branched off in the thirteenth century. The Austrian dukes more wisely governed their states in common, and, by happy marriages, so greatly increased the bulk of them as to become far the most important house in Germany. The Luxemburg people also had the wisdom to keep their estates together.

It should also be mentioned that the house of Hohenzollern, which had begun with the burggraviate of Nuremberg, by strict attachment to Lewis of Bavaria, in whose hereditary estates that imperial city was situated, made a great step towards the acquisition of both territory and dignity, although it was nearly a century still before they were to attain the electorate of Brandenburg.

Switzerland.—Another point to be noticed is the attitude of the Swiss. I have already mentioned the original
league formed against the Hapsburg supremacy, and the
recognition of the freedom of Uri, Schwiz, and Unterwalden by Henry VII. Fortunately for them the interests
of Lewis led him to repeat the favour to protect the
cantons as imperial dependencies against their common
enemies, the dukes of Austria. Encouraged by his
approval, if not strengthened with his assistance, the
cantons overthrew Duke Leopold at Morgarten in 1315,
the result of the victory being the change of a temporary
alliance into a perpetual federation. For many years
the Austrian dukes had other work than the subjugation
of the Swiss: a truce for six years was concluded in
1318; when that expired, they fought for Lewis against
Leopold until 1326.

In 1332 the three cantons received Lucerne into the
federation, to the manifest loss of Austria, which had
rights in Lucerne that she had not elsewhere. Later on,
in the reign of Lewis, in 1335 and 1338, quite independently of the Forest Cantons, another centre of freedom
was created in two other parts of what now is Switzerland. Both in Zürich and in Bern the municipal or
popular families began a struggle against the feudal
nobility, which, within and without the walls, threatened
or oppressed them. The struggle of the imperial cities
was not, like that of the Forest Cantons, against the house
of Austria ; they came into collision almost immediately
with the imperial government. The battle of Laupen in
1339, won by the help of the Forest Cantons against the
imperial and feudal forces, settled the liberty of Bern.
The struggle of Zurich runs on into the next reign : it
was not until 1353 that the league of eight cantons was
established. Uri, Schwiz, and Unterwalden formed the

original confederation of 1308, which was increased by
the adhesion of Lucerne, which was emancipated from
Austria in 1332, of Bern, whose battle they had fought at
Laupen, of Zürich, whose cause they had adopted in
1357, and of Zug and Glarus, which they had conquered
and liberated from Austria in the same year. The final
acquisition of Tyrol by Austria in 1362 gave her another
point of attack upon Switzerland, and the interest of the
struggle after that period becomes more complicated.

The Hanseatic League.—In all this strife of dynasties
and in all these struggles of new communities for liberty,
we ought not to forget the spreading power of the
Hanseatic league in the north of Germany, nor, too, the
mercantile enterprise and independence of the imperial
towns, such as Augsburg and Nuremberg in the south.
We know that they were at work; that, by the
title of imperial towns, they meant an independence
almost republican; emancipation from all extraneous
rule of count or bishop; and dependence only on the
far off, and weak, central power, which was too remote
to meddle with them against their will. Fortunately they
were well able both to pay their way and to fight their
battles. Especially the rich and noble cities of Westphalia, with their manufactures and commerce, their
strong walls, and their magnificent churches, clung to
the Bavarian king, and, under the shadow of his distant
eagles, vindicated their liberty against alien encroachments. Besides the towns, however, there was another
organisation gathering great strength on the north-eastern
borders of Germany, winning from heathenism and
barbarism a country which was not yet German; namely,
the Teutonic and Livonian orders of knighthood, which
kept up the spirit of the crusades until they had founded
a strong state on the frontier, a state destined to give

name and power, after a couple of centuries, to the house of Hohenzollern, and two centuries later to a new kingdom, that of Prussia. At present their exploits only indirectly touch Germany.

Lewis IV. and John of Bohemia.—Lewis of Bavaria has the credit of having devoted his time, when he had any, to his own people. He found it better and pleasanter, when he had peace, to live in Bavaria than to go about, as his predecessors had done, to the various imperial estates, living on their revenues like the wandering kings of old. He lived in his hereditary lands; for their improvement he laboured; and for them he legislated. His code of Bavarian laws was intended to ameliorate the difficulties of the old unintelligible system; for, of all points of German history, the most inscrutable, to any but a German lawyer, is the question how the laws of the kingdom were made, amended, or executed.

In strong contrast with Lewis stands that erratic genius, that most mischievous wandering star, John of Bohemia, whose vagaries are hardly worth puzzling over, but are the key to much of the complication of a reign, giving to him an importance of which he is anything but deserving. His death at Creçy, to most readers, covers the multitude of his sins, but not to one who studies the life and grieves over the misery of Germany.

IMPORTANT DATES

Lewis of Bavaria, 1314–1347.
Battle of Morgarten, 1315.
Battle of Muhldorf, 1322.
Lewis is proclaimed emperor at Milan, 1327.
Lewis is crowned at Rome, 1327.
Lewis joins Edward III., 1338.
Lewis excommunicated by Clement VII., 1346.

CHAPTER VII

Charles IV.—Günther of Schwartzburg—The Golden Bull—Its provisions—Its significance—The Tyrol—His rule in Germany—Crowned King of Arles, 1365—Relations with England and France—His character.

The Death of Lewis IV. an Epoch.—With Lewis of Bavaria closes a period, not of great interest for Germany, especially, but of very much greater than the one that follows it, and which extends from the accession of Charles IV. to the reign of Sigismund, if not longer. During this period we mark the increase and extension of all the characteristics of weakness, that have manifested themselves in German life, since the revival under Rudolf of Hapsburg; we mark the same tendency, enormously exaggerated, of entire submission to the papacy; we mark the same dereliction of the duties of the empire in Italy; duties which, however foreign to the true character of a German king, were attached most certainly to his historical position, as claiming the succession of the Cæsars, of Charles the Great, the Ottos, Henry III., and Frederick I.; and we mark how the whole energy of the ruler centres upon the aggrandisement of his house, or the benefit of his hereditary dominions, to the neglect of the rest of the kingdom. This was the policy, not of Charles IV. only, but of the age which he represented.

Lewis of Bavaria had humiliated himself to the pope, and had devoted himself far more to the cultivation of his hereditary domains, and the increase of his family influence, than to the regulation of Germany. But he had not neglected Germany, until he found that action was, for him, hampered everywhere by the papal excommunication, almost an impossibility; and it was by his resolute attempt to vindicate his imperial rights in Italy, deserted by the pope, and disorganised to the last degree by the quarrels of the native nobles ' and the threatening and undermining policy of the French, that he, if he did not incur, at least rendered inexorable, that pertinacious hostility on the part of the pope, to which he finally succumbed. But Charles IV. never risked his friendly relations with the papacy by showing a spark of independence. As for the empire, it came, in all matters, second to his own kingdom and the interests of the house of Luxemburg. Into Italy he never ventured, but as a private person, except on the occasion of his coronation, after which he was obliged to subside again—was not suffered to remain even a single night in Rome.

The Emperor Charles IV.—Never, perhaps, were German influences so small in the general politics of Europe, although, had they been greater than they were, they might not have been listened to in the great struggle between France and England, that continued during the whole of Charles's reign. And yet, with all this, no prince ever made more of the externals of empire; no emperor yet had reigned so long without an anti-Cæsar; no emperor legislated more definitely for the framework of the empire, or obtained a wider recognition for the rights of the central authority, although the recognition, safe enough, and readily enough vouchsafed, since he would have been utterly unable to make it a reality, generally ended in words or in pompous ceremonies. He proclaimed peace, and made strict regulations for it, but

he could not execute it !   He was crowned at Rome under
orthodox circumstances, but he had not even the show
of respect paid him there.   He was crowned King of
Arles, but all that his royal title gave him was freedom
to confirm all the encroachments that for a hundred
and fifty years the policy of France, the weakness of
the empire, and the practical independence of the native
nobles of that kingdom had created.   And yet, with all
this, he managed better than many a better man ; left
the imperial system (or so much of it as subsisted
at all) much sounder than he found it ; for peace, or
rather the absence of any general division—such as had
been going on in former reigns between pope and Cæsar,
Cæsar and anti-Cæsar, or between north and south, or
Bavaria and Austria—gave the whole nation breathing
time, and time of growth to all institutions that had the
elements of growth in them, such as the imperial cities
and the mercantile leagues.

Charles is called by historians "the father of Bohemia,
and the stepfather of Germany"; a name, true perhaps in the main, because, although Germany did
profit somewhat under his government, it was always
secondary to Bohemia in his thought, and it was his
policy for Bohemia and Luxemburg which inclined him
to the line he took and kept as touching the empire.
The reign, however, cannot be called unimportant,
though it is not interesting.

With Italy we have indeed little to do ; the romantic
episode of Rienzi concerns Charles very little as a man,
very much less as an emperor : whoever wishes to
understand it, and much besides that is interesting in
the condition of Rome, must read it in Gregorovius,
or, more easily, in Milman, who has devoted to it, *con
amore*, one of the most charming chapters of his book,

writing from materials undiscovered when Gibbon made out of the same one of the most charming chapters of his. Nor does the rest of the foreign policy of Charles contain much that calls for detailed notice. His connection is with France, as Lewis of Bavaria's had been with England, but it was a relation not of warlike alliance, only of friendship and peace. France had other enemies to fight, and Charles had no strength on this side of Europe to undertake to be her champion. On the other side, his relations towards Poland and Hungary were more significant.

His Character.—Personally, Charles is not a favourite with historians; he is said to have resembled in appearance the Slavonic family from which his mother sprang, and this was not likely to make him attractive to the Germans; he was certainly the very antithesis of his father, the bold, inconstant, presumptuous knight-errant. If his bad qualities were in the other extreme from those of his father, so certainly were they non-German: low cunning, meanness and subterfuge, the suspicion of darker expedients, when it was necessary to get a troublesome adversary out of the way, are distinctly non-German. These, however, are not common characteristics among the Slavonic races.

In the last chapter we left Charles running away from Creçy, where he had lost his troublesome, unmanageable father, and succeeded to a kingdom, more solid and certain than the one which he was claiming against Lewis. Lewis, we saw, survived about a year, both the election of the anti-Cæsar and the battle of Creçy. But the death of Lewis did not leave the field entirely open to Charles; the feeling in Germany against French and papal influence was very strong, and the sons and kinsmen of Lewis in the Palatinate, Holland, Brandenburg, Bavaria, and the Tyrol were not prepared for unconditional submission. The papal policy, moreover, in the deposition of the Archbishop of Mainz, had given a head to the other party and increased the difficulty of ensuring an undisputed election.

Opposition to his Election.—The electors who had chosen Charles in 1346 were his kinsman, Baldwin of Trèves, the Archbishop of Cologne, the intrusive Archbishop of Mainz, one of the rival dukes of Saxony, and his own father, King John: five out of the seven; but out of the five two with questioned or questionable rights. Opposed to him were now the Elector Palatine, the Margrave of Brandenburg, son of Lewis, Eric of Lauenburg, and Henry of Luneburg. These were really the weaker party in the present condition of Germany, and Charles had obtained recognition among the princes whilst they were deliberating. The opposing electors met in person or by deputy at Lahnstein in January 1348, and agreed to offer the crown to Edward III. of England, who had been imperial vicar in the west under Lewis, and who was now realising the fruits of his victory at Creçy. Edward had seen too much of Lewis's troubles to be anxious to take his place. He declined at once. They then applied to Frederick, Margrave of Meissen, in June, the town of Nuremberg being very anxious for his election; that voice probably representing the interests of the imperial cities. Frederick, however, showed his sympathy with the mercantile spirit, by accepting 10,000 marks from Charles, and keeping quiet. Lewis of Brandenburg was himself thought of; but he was not strong enough for the place; and the fourth person chosen, Günther of Schwartzburg, who was elected on January 30, 1349, accepted, on condition that it should be shown that the throne was really vacant. Having accepted, he proceeded to Frankfort with a large force, and there, after a siege of six weeks, he was at last received as king.

Charles Successful.—Charles prepared also for war. Günther took up his position at Frankfort; Charles at Mainz. But the question was decided without a battle. Günther was poisoned by his physician, or some one who had planned the destruction of both of them, for the physician himself perished by a dose of the same medicine; Günther's life was prolonged by a timely antidote for a few months, but his health was entirely ruined, and Charles left no means untried to draw off his friends. Lewis of Brandenburg was the first to go, the offer of a plenary restitution and investiture of the possessions that his father had given him was too much for him. He was so far honest, however, to Günther, that he concluded terms between him and Charles (Trinity Sunday, June 7). Günther accepted 20,000 marks, which Charles raised by pawning imperial domains, and, complaining bitterly of the desertion of the Bavarians, died a few days after at Frankfort of the effects of the poison (June 19, 1349). Charles, who was credited with the guilt of the poisoning, attended his funeral.

Charles was now the sole aspirant; he had got rid of his enemies. Henceforth he reigned without a rival. From this date to 1354 we see him travelling about Germany, arranging quarrels among the princes and between the cities and their lords. In Brandenburg, a false Waldemar appeared, pretending to be the margrave who died in 1318; and the duke, Rudolf of Saxony, the representative of the old Ballenstadt or Ascanian house of Brandenburg, made his claim to complicate matters more. Lewis purchased Charles's help by surrendering the care of the imperial insignia; but he shortly after resigned to his younger brother, Lewis the Roman, and retired into Bavaria. Charles after this published a general peace at Spires (1354), and shortly after the rivalry at Mainz was extinguished by the death of Henry of Luneburg and the peaceful succession of the papal nominee.

I anticipated in the last chapter the little bit of Swiss history which fills the interval between the pacification of 1351 and the Italian expedition of 1354. Charles entered Italy with a small retinue in September in that year; and, carrying peace with him, confirming the privileges of every one who asked him, and carefully avoiding anything that could make him enemies, reached Milan, and received the iron crown there on the Epiphany, 1355. At Rome, on Easter Day, he was crowned by the Bishop of Ostia, representing Pope Innocent VI.; and, as it was only on this condition that he was so honoured, rejecting the petitions of the Romans. He had to set out the same day on his return to Pisa, and thence, after a narrow escape for his life from fire, to Prague, and so into Germany.

The Golden Bull, 1356.—Immediately after his coronation, in conformity with a practice that afterwards became a piece of imperial etiquette, he had summoned a diet at Nuremberg on the feast of St. Martin, and then and there (January 10) published the first part of the Golden Bull, in 23 Articles; completing it by the addition of the remaining ones in a similar assembly at Metz at Christmas 1356.

This Golden Bull, although it contained little that was new, was a very important act, for it settled the constitution of the electoral body for the remaining years of the empire, and, in some measure, is entitled to be called the Constitution, or the first written exposition of the Constitution of Germany. In this view it really does sum up, and make presentable, many of the results of movements which have been described in previous chapters.

The Golden Bull begins with a somewhat rhapsodic effusion in praise of unity, which is not out of place considering the object of the act. It contains after this preamble thirty articles, twenty-three of which were published at Nuremberg, and the rest at Metz.

Art. 1 provides for the safe conduct of the electors to Frankfort on the occasion of the election of the King of the Romans, and enumerates the princes who are to be answerable for the safe escort of each to the place of meeting. The Archbishop of Mainz is to issue letters of summons, within a month of the vacancy, and the electors are to meet within three months of the summons. No prince elector is to bring with him more than two hundred horse, or fifty men-at-arms.

Art. 2 orders the ceremony of election, the oath to be administered by the Archbishop of Mainz; the electors are not to quit Frankfort until the election is made, and, after thirty days, if a decision is not arrived at, they are to be put on a diet of bread and water. Further, when the election is made, the person elect is to confirm all the rights, privileges, and immunities of the electors before he can do any other act. An absolute majority of votes is to decide, and, if three electors present shall elect a fourth who is absent, their votes, the four altogether, shall be regarded as a clear majority.

Art. 3 orders the position of the ecclesiastical electors in the diet. The Archbishop of Trèves sits opposite the emperor. Cologne and Mainz, on the left or right, according to the province or chancery in which the

diet is held.   Art. 4: The prince electors are to sit,
Bohemia next but one to the king on the right, and next
to him the Count Palatine; Saxony and Brandenburg
in the same way on the left.   The Archbishop of Mainz
is to collect the votes; the Archbishop of Trèves is to
give the first, Cologne the second; then, in order,
Bohemia, the Count Palatine, Saxony, and Brandenburg.
The grand serjeanties of the electors are also specified.
Art. 5 makes the Count Palatine vicar, in a vacancy,
of the Rhine country, Swabia, and Franconia; the Duke
of Saxony in the districts under Saxon law.   The Count
Palatine is judge in all cases in which the King of the
Romans is a defendant.   Art. 6 provides for the maintenance of the precedence of the electors.   Art. 7
confirms the right of primogeniture and of feudal succession generally and specifically in the electorates.
Arts. 8, 9, 10 concern Bohemia; the immunities of
the people from foreign jurisdiction; the right of the
king in mines and dues; and the right of coinage.
Art. 11 exempts the subjects of the electors from the
jurisdiction of external courts, except in case of denial
of justice where there is an appeal direct to the imperial
court.   Art. 12: The electors are to assemble every
year at Easter for a month: during which no public
entertainments are to be given for fear of wasting time
and money.   Art. 13 revokes all imperial acts deroga-
tory to the privileges of the electors.   Art. 14 forbids the
illusory renunciation of fiefs, made by vassals defying
their lords.   Art. 15 forbids leagues and conspiracies,
especially amongst the cities—a sign of the times; Art.
16: the illusory creation of *Pfahlburgers*, or denizens,
by whose pretended emancipation their lords lose their
feudal rights.   Art. 17 restricts and regulates the right
of defiance or challenge which had been allowed by

I

Frederick Barbarossa, in order to check the ravages committed in private wars, and was not finally abolished until the reign of Maximilian.

Arts. 18, 19 are the forms of summons and proxy for an election. Art. 20 forbids the division of the territory to which the electoral vote belongs, and thus precludes family quarrels about the vote, such as had prevailed and injured the validity of election in the houses of Saxony and Bavaria. Arts. 21, 22, 23 order the precedence of the electors in procession and at Mass. The remaining articles were published at Metz, December 25, 1356. Art. 24 contains the punishments for conspiracy against the electors; they are the punishments of treason. Art. 25 amplifies Art. 20 on the indivisibility of the electoral domain. Arts. 26, 27, 28, 29 define the ceremonies which are to be performed at the holding of an imperial court; the precedence of the princes, the functions and perquisites of the King of Bohemia as cup-bearer, Count Palatine as steward, Saxony as marshal, and Brandenburg as chamberlain; the arrangement of the tables at the feast; the place of the election, Frankfort; the coronation, Aix-la-Chapelle; the first court, Nuremberg.

The last article, No. 30, directs that the prince electors shall take pains to have their children instructed from the age of seven years in the four languages which are spoken in the empire—Latin, German, Italian, and Slavonic: a conclusion which is more practical and probably more useful and important than nine-tenths of the elaborate programme that preceded it.

Conclusions.—The natural conclusion to draw from this very curious document is that the empire had become, as to jurisdiction, a confederation of electoral princes, with an occasional appeal to the emperor in extreme cases.

The imperial jurisdiction has ceased in the dominions
of the electors, except by way of appeal; the feudal
system of government in those territories has, except
in that single point, eliminated the very idea of a central
jurisdiction. No directions are given as to the estates
of princes and prelates which do not fall under the
electorates; but in these cases there was, it seems, very
little more of reality left to the imperial officers; even
in the imperial cities, these officers had become hereditary nobles, and were ousted from jurisdiction by the
successive charters that confirmed the independent,
internal management of the cities. On the one side
the emperor was bought out by his friends, on the other
he was driven out by his enemies.

What little he had to do in Germany generally seems
to be reduced to the holding of an imperial court, and
perhaps to the ineffectual proclamations of peace. He
was the impersonation of an idea of nationality, which
might be felt or not, but was very rarely acted on, and
which had little other sentiment or policy, or common
object. We might liken him to the honorary president
of a knightly order, but that the grand-masters of
the orders at this period wielded far more power and
patronage than he.

We see from the careful provisions made in the
Golden Bull, for Bohemia, which really occupies a far
more prominent position in it than is required, except
for the fact that it is Charles's own kingdom, that his
hereditary kingdom came first in his thoughts, and that
the maintenance of its rights, precedence, and possessions as an electorate, was quite as important to him
as the protection of the dignity of the King of the
Romans. But no doubt the settling of the territory
and indivisibilty of the electorates, and the extinction

of the disputes as to votes, was the great benefit involved in the measure. Henceforth, Brandenburg and Saxony were obliged to attach the vote to the possession of a distinct and indivisible domain.[1]

Bavaria.—The question between Bohemia and Bavaria was settled, as it had been by Rudolf and Adolf, in favour of the former. The question between Bavaria and the Palatinate, which had been determined by Lewis of Bavaria, in the shape of an alternate vote, was settled summarily against Bavaria. The Electoral College required and received no more modification until the balance of power was readjusted in the sixteenth century. So much, then, for the Golden Bull, which brings us down to the Christmas of the year 1356.

The transactions of the few following years are unimportant; a little war in Bavaria, in which the emperor forced the dukes to peace; a little war in Swabia, ended by an arbitration at Nuremberg between the towns of Swabia and the Counts of Würtemberg, by which the former were freed from the *advocatia*, their burdensome and expensive relations to the latter; the birth and magnificent christening of Wenzel, the future king—these are nearly all that the historians have to tell us of the events of German history to 1361. Probably the ravages of the Black Death, and the paralysis of anything like political or other combinations under that terrible scourge, had the effect of producing something like stagnation.

---

[1] "Charles," writes Professor Lodge in "The Close of the Middle Ages," p. 118, "was profoundly convinced . . . that the medieval empire was at an end, and that any attempt to revive it would result in the ruin of Germany." He continues on p. 119: "His (Charles') intention was to obtain for the house of Luxemburg such an overwhelming territorial strength that he would secure to his successors a practically hereditary claim to the imperial office." Charles hoped "to build up a territorial monarchy like that which existed in England, and was in process of construction in France."

In this year, 1361, we come on the event that determined the duration of the little attempt made by Bavaria
to acquire a more influential position territorially in
Germany—the collapse of the family policy of Lewis
of Bavaria. In 1361 died Lewis the elder, the son of
Lewis of Bavaria, to whom he had given Brandenburg,
and for whom he had detached Margaret Maultasch
from her Bohemian or Luxemburgish husband (John
Henry of Moravia), bringing down on himself merely
the hostility of both the pope and King John. Lewis
had before this resigned Brandenburg to his younger
brother, and retired into Bavaria, where he lived on his
own portion of the inheritance, and administered the
Tyrol in the name of his wife and infant son. His death
was followed in a very short time by his son Meinhard's;
his portion of Bavaria reverted to the general stock, but
the Tyrol was ceded by Margaret to the Duke of Austria
in 1363; and ever since the donation, except for a short
time during the wars of the Revolution, the Tyrol has
continued to belong to the house of Hapsburg, at once
the most faithful and the most impregnable portion of
their dominions.

Brandenburg.—A few years later Lewis the Roman, to
whom his brother had surrendered Brandenburg, died
(1365), and Otto, another son of the old emperor Lewis,
succeeded. But he felt that the emperor, by his position
as King of Bohemia in Moravia, and by his influence as
emperor with the princes of Meissen, was edging him out
of all authority; whilst the attacks of Pomerania on the
north, against which Charles should have defended him,
made his life a burden to him, and he accordingly, with the
consent of his family, sold the Electorate to Charles in
1373. There was an *Erbverbrüderung* between the houses
of Luxemburg and Brandenburg, with reference to this

electorate, as we saw at Charles's accession, which Otto, vexed with Charles's behaviour, attempted to unsettle in favour of his nephew, Frederick of Bavaria. The emperor attempted to oust him, but the matter was, in that year (1373), settled by a money payment and an abdication. The emperor immediately appointed his son Wenzel elector, thus adding a large territory to the estates of his family, a territory lying extremely convenient for the objects of their ambition towards Poland, and indeed Hungary likewise.

Thus, then, ended the latest of the three attempts, the first being that of Austria, and the second that of Luxemburg, to acquire power by amassing without consolidating large territories in the hands of a single family.

The Later Years of Charles IV. His Death, 1378.—In 1365 Charles was crowned King of Arles. He had already performed some acts of sovereignty—in particular, he had confirmed the sale of Avignon made by Joanna of Naples to the pope in 1348,[1] and had appointed his uncle, Baldwin, Archbishop of Trèves, vicar and guardian of the kingdom of Arles. But these acts, like most of his imperial ones, were very perfunctory, and all that he took by his coronation seems to have been the right to recognise a state of things which he could not alter.

In 1367 he joined with a large Bohemian force a papal expedition against the Visconti (acting in this matter as a simple ally), but after a few skirmishes allowed himself to be bought off, and returned to Bohemia. In 1368 he visited Rome, and had the empress crowned by Pope Urban V. He then returned through Lombardy, receiving, it is said, large sums of money from the cities

---

[1] Avignon sold to the pope for 80,000 gold florins in 1348.

on various accounts. In all the rest of his dealings with Italy he seems to have accepted the rôle of a papal lieutenant, and to have really done nothing to vindicate his title as emperor. Matters glided on until 1376: private wars continuing, and constant leagues being formed by the cities, in spite of the Golden Bull, and in spite, likewise, of constant attempts of the emperor to mediate. He cannot be accused of neglect of duty in this respect: he made frequent long journeys, and held magnificent courts in the cities he visited; and often by the prestige of his name and the adroitness of his management he was able to prevent and make up quarrels. Now he was getting old, that is, about sixty, and he wished to see Wenzel elected King of the Romans before he died. Gregory XI., with some difficulty, he persuaded to allow this, for this time only. To induce the electors to consent he had to offer enormous bribes, and as he could not pay them, he pawned to them the scanty remains of imperial domain that he still held.

After these preparations the election was held on June 10, 1376; the coronation followed on July 6, and an embassy was then sent to Pope Gregory for confirmation. The pope deferred the confirmation on the pretence of the youth of Wenzel, who was not yet seventeen, and he died, in fact, before confirming him. A disputed election to the papacy followed, and the great western schism in consequence. Urban VI., the pope elected under the pressure of the Roman people, and in opposition to the policy and influence of France, hastened to make himself a friend by the confirmation of Wenzel. This determined the position of Germany during the schism.

Although Charles was in reality attached to France, and had never, in the course of a long reign, had more than a passing difficulty with the house of Valois, he, at once propitiated by the action of the pope, threw his weight into the Italian scale. The patronage by the French of the antipope at Avignon, threw the English into the party of Urban; and this coincidence, for at the time it was little more, drew the English and Germans together in a very important way, and produced an amount of common action between them, and even personal acquaintance and friendship between their kings, that had been long unknown.

These matters belong rather to the next three reigns. For the present, Pope Urban's recognition of Wenzel was gratefully returned by Charles, who recognised him as Catholic pope. The rest of Germany followed, but Savoy, Lorraine, and Bar, and some other border counties, where imperial influence was weak, and the French in close neighbourhood, recognised Clement. The Scots recognised the French pope, and hence the curious results in English politics, by which the royal and opposition parties were enabled to get rid of the bishops opposed to them. But Italy, Hungary, Poland, and Portugal supported Urban, and it was only by great art and diplomatic ability that Spain was prevented from doing the same. Charles IV. died, however, soon after the beginning of the schism, at Prague, on November 29, 1378.

Character of Charles IV.—If Charles were not guilty of the poisoning of Günther of Schwarzburg, we may study his character without disgust; if he were, then the character loses any redeeming tinge that integrity, otherwise exemplified or taken for granted, can give it. Charles was a tolerably successful man; but he was of a low type and stamp, and his success was not such as gratifies a wise or sound mind. He has had many imitators, conscious or unconscious, among more modern kings; he was, perhaps, weak-minded, an inferior mentally, but in the same line, and comparatively innocuous specimen of the order that is represented by Lewis XI. of France. But setting aside his personal character, his meanness, cunning, and petty ambition, I should be loth to say that his reign was an unfortunate one for Germany. Inglorious as were his transactions with Italy and the papacy, and humiliating as were his relations to the latter, still the state of peace which they ensured was for the time more beneficial to Germany than the more heroic position that he might have claimed, involving the constant drain of blood and treasure, or the constant interchange of excommunications and depositions which were generally the result of a bolder policy. Nor should we forget the lesson which all along the reading of German history teaches, of the baneful result of the connection with Italy. For the character of emperor and hero it would no doubt be better that a man should insist on and fight for the vindication of his claims there; but for the German nation it would have been well that Italy should have sunk under the sea, or been blown up with her own volcanoes. The slightness of the imperial connection with Italy was a security to Germany. The lull of imperial warfare there, implied peace and a breathing space.

It is impossible to say that all these benefits resulted from Charles's Italian policy of abstinence; for the prevalence of private war in Germany seems to have been as great as ever; but there was no disruption, no great party warfare, nor anything like a general armament in Germany during the thirty-one years of his reign. His own energetic attempts at peace, one of the strongest proofs of any strength that his character might possess. One or two of his other administrative acts may be mentioned. He issued, in 1348, a constitutional edict in Bohemia, allowing the states to elect a king of Bohemia in case the royal family should become extinct (an ordinance which, as we saw, formed part of the Golden Bull); he thus exempts his hereditary kingdom from the usual risks of a feudal dependency, whilst he as clearly as possible lays the way open for the Thirty Years' War. In 1349 he raised the Counts of Mecklenburg to the rank of dukes. In 1354 he did the same for the Count of Bar; in 1356 for the Count of Jülich. The most important act of the kind in its distant results, which he did, was the elevation of the burgraves of Nuremberg, the Hohenzollerns, that is, to the rank of princes of the empire, which was done in 1363.

His Marriages.—Charles was four times married. His first wife was a sister of Philip of Valois, married in 1333. His second Anna, daughter of Rudolf, the Count Palatine, 1349; the third also Anna, daughter of Henry, Duke of Schweidnitz, 1353 to 1364, and the fourth Elizabeth of Pomerania, in 1365. He had many daughters, whom he married with a view to the strengthening of the family. Of his sons, Wenzel, the son of the third wife, and Sigismund, son of the fourth, became kings of the Romans; of the daughters the one who interests us most was Anna (by the fourth wife), the first wife of Richard II. of England, whom she married in 1382, and over whom her influence for good is said or supposed to have been great. She bore the title of the Good Queen Anne, and died in 1396; after her death her husband's follies and troubles consequent on them, developed fearfully and fatally; and she has by tradition the reputation of having been the link somehow between the Lollards and Wycliffites of England and the anti-papal and anti-German religionists of Bohemia, of whom we shall hear so much under Sigismund.

The Luxemburg Emperors.—The study of the character of the Luxemburg house is interesting. In Henry VII. we have the thorough old German hero ; as brave as a knight-errant, and as wise as an old politician. In John of Bohemia you get the knight-errantry exaggerated, and the wisdom, if not altogether eliminated, continuing only in the shape of guile. In Charles IV. the knight-errant is eliminated, and the guile exaggerated into unscrupulous policy. In Wenzel you get the erratic characteristics of his grandfather developed into absolute insanity under the influence of a mind altogether undisciplined and depraved by drunkenness. Sigismund, on the other hand, seems to reunite all the characteristics. There is a great dash of the knight-errant and adventurer : going in for half a dozen kingdoms ; rushing about the world crusading and fighting the Turks ; or visiting the remotest parts of Europe as his own ambassador. He is a John of Bohemia over again. Next we see him holding councils of the Church, with all the pomp and circumstance of Charles IV.; laying down his law as head of the state of Europe and principal agent of the council that supersedes the pope. The king of the Romans and emperor, in his own mind, if in no one else's; and not only *super-grammaticam,* according to the story, but above common sense as well. But, with all his absurdities, his adventurousness and his policies, there is a touch of honesty and sincerity occasionally about him which brings him nearer to Henry VII. than to any of his intermediate ancestors.

Charles IV., then, left three sons—Wenzel, already elected to be King of the Romans, Sigismund, who became, on his father's death, Margrave of Brandenburg, in 1386 King of Hungary, King of the Romans in 1410, King of Bohemia in 1419, of Lombardy in 1431, and emperor in 1433. John of Gorlitz, the third son, was provided for in Lusatia and the neighbouring Slavonian regions.

The Slavs.—Charles IV. wrote his own life; it only reaches, however, to the year 1346, and cannot be made to throw much light on German history, although it may on Bohemia and on the personal relations of Charles in his younger days. The relations into which the Sclavonic connection brings Germany, her share in the politics of Hungary and Poland, begin with John and Charles to assume their modern form; and in it an influence hardly less marked than that which earlier has been felt from the Italian connection.

How greatly Austrian and through Austria German interests have been and are still affected by the Slavonic neighbourhood, and by the fact that the crowns of Hungary and Bohemia have for centuries rested on the head of the elect emperor, can only be realised by a study of modern history down to the present day. All that is historical in these relations begins with the Luxemburg family, and is transmitted by them to the Austrian. In these days (1883), when the old Slavonic spirit is rising, and partly Latin, partly Greek in religion, is hesitating between Austria and Russia as the protector of pan-Slavic unity, we may yet live to see some strange results even from the policy of Charles IV.

IMPORTANT DATES

Charles IV., 1347–1378.
The Golden Bull, 1356.
Peace with the Swiss, 1358.
Charles visits Rome, 1368.
Wenzel elected King of the Romans, 1376.

CHAPTER VIII

The End of the Fourteenth Century.—If ever there was
a period at which it might fairly be said that
monarchy in Europe had worn out its mission, and,
whether the world were ripe for a change or not, it
at least must be put out of the way, it was, I think, the
last quarter of the fourteenth century. In the first place
there were two popes; one, Urban VI. (1378 to 1389),
a monster of cruelty and tyranny, in whom his contemporaries saw nothing but the suspicion of madness
to excuse him; the other (Clement VII.), a mere agent
of France and French interests, more respectable, but
as unfit to moderate in the councils of Europe, and in
the countries opposed to him regarded not merely as a
schismatic but as a heretic; for as such Wycliffe con-
tinually treats him. After Urban came Boniface IX., the
political tool of conflicting alternations of party.

Richard II., Charles VI., and Wenzel.—In England
we have the boy king, Richard II., spoilt by his
guardians, kept back from public business, and driven
in upon private excesses and extravagances until they
have become a second nature to him, to develop, in
spite of natural ability and noble instincts, into what
was, to all intents and purposes, an insane attempt

at tyranny as the only source of revenge and form of real power. In France we have the unfortunate Charles VI., not merely, like Richard, liable to a suspicion of insanity, but actually stark mad, and his kingdom for many years ruined by the results of his malady. In Italy there is the terrible tragedy of Queen Johanna (murdered in 1382), followed up by a double succession of claimants, persecuting one another; Charles of Durazzo expiating the murder of Johanna by his equally tragic murder in Hungary; Elizabeth of Hungary, his murderess, falling a victim in her turn. And in Germany, where one might have hoped at least for something like a centre of gravity and an escape from the madness and misery that is all around, what do we find but King Wenzel, if not as mad as his brother kings, disqualified by mad drunkenness from ever doing justice to that discreet and penetrating judgment which, according to the German historians, he possessed but could only show when he was sober.

Condition of European Politics.—I do not mean, of course, that all these calamities fell on European society at exactly the same time. Pope Urban VI. concluded his savage career in 1389, and Charles of France did not fall a victim to his disease until 1392; but the unsettled state of England continued throughout the period, and Wenzel seems, so far as we know, to have been drunk all the time! The result of the reaction following the enormous exertions made by France and England earlier in the century was to produce throughout great part of Europe an uneasy peace. The war between England and France was carried on indeed, but for years only nominally, neither people rising to an effort; France and Germany were undisturbed in their relations, as indeed they generally were under the Luxemburgs; in Italy there was constant bloodshed; in Hungary there was constant bloodshed; in Germany there were constant defiances and private wars, but there was no national war, unless the quarrels of the Italians among themselves, and the revolutions and party struggles between Sicily and Naples, or their rulers, can be taken to wear the dimensions of such a struggle.

General Characteristics.—There are, however, some few characteristics which cannot be passed over. There is, first of all, and throughout all, an amount of cruel capricious bloodshed, unparalleled at any period of the history of Christendom. In England there is the vindictive proceeding of the Lords Appellant against the king's favourites in 1387, and the equally cruel reprisals of Richard in 1397; not to speak of the very suspicious circumstances of Gloucester's death. In Italy there is the persecution by Urban VI. of the suspected cardinals, the torture of the unhappy old men, and their final disappearance, undoubtedly by secret execution. In France there come, shortly after the period closes, but thoroughly of a piece with it, the mortal feuds between Orleans and Burgundy, and a little later the massacre of the Armagnacs. At Naples there is the murder of Queen Johanna, and the long list of reprisals falling, with an awful poetry of justice, rapidly after one another. In the dominion of Wenzel, as we shall see, there was not less innocent, noble, and sacred blood spilt, than elsewhere.

This is a new characteristic: of wars, rebellions, tumults, there have been enough in the ruder ages, but now that civilisation advances, now that the unreality of a revived chivalry, which never existed but in theory, forms the outward manners of society, come these secret murders, poisonings, thirst for political bloodshed.

Under such a state of governmental morality we cannot wonder at a second point that is worth noting: the policy of combination among individuals, and between communities, by which it was attempted to supply through a voluntary confederation that security and guarantee of order which ought to have been furnished by the Government. In England and France this had shown itself in the revolt of the Commons and in the wars of the Jacquerie, and for want of organisation only had failed to effect a revolution. But in Germany as in Switzerland, and at an earlier period in Italy, it took the form of leagues and confederations between city and city, or cities and nobles, or cities and princes; the princes themselves forming themselves into societies, half like orders of chivalry, half like allied powers, and sharing in some degree the features of the old Vehmic Society which itself revived.

A third point I will notice is, the extension of this principle of superseding ineffective or bad government by voluntary association, in religious matters; a development from causes which had been long at work, such as the preaching of the friars, the doctrines of the mystics, and reaction from the excesses of the strict Franciscans, but which in the schism of the papacy, the general disorganisation of society, and the spread of the idea of voluntary association, assumed a character, under the Wycliffites and the Hussites, which was to help to determine religious changes in Europe for all time to come.

Wenzel's Reign.—From this preface you will probably infer that I shall throw the history of Wenzel into some

K

form corresponding with these heads : his cruelties, the combinations of the cities and princes, and the progress of revolutionary principles in religious matters. In truth the personal adventures of Wenzel, grotesque as many of them are, and still more grotesque as they are represented by the later historians, whose narratives seem to be melting away before modern criticism, only indirectly touch the history of Germany. Germany he left very much at her own disposal. An occasional diet, or an occasional confirmation of privileges ; or the occasional bestowal of imperial sanction on a league ; or a spasmodic effort now and then to arbitrate between the popes, nearly complete all that can be said of the German life of Wenzel. In Bohemia, where he lived, he was always in difficulties, and there his adventures occur chiefly.

There can be no doubt, all things considered, that Wenzel was one of the most worthless creatures that ever were called kings. There have been worse kings, perhaps, that is, men whose wickedness has done more harm to their subjects, but scarcely one in whom there is so little of anything admirable to redeem the blank stupidity of his vice. The only element of life there is in his history is the capricious madness of his crimes. His career in Bohemia is one long quarrel with the nobles of that country, whom he would have been glad simply to exterminate.

Having set Prague against him, he fortified himself a castle in the neighbourhood, where he took refuge whenever the popular spirit was too strong for him, and thence conducted his ravages. Early in his reign he brought in the Free companies to put down the national opposition, and thus assisted to devastate his own kingdom. His acts of cruelty culminated in 1389 in the attempt to massacre the whole of the

Bohemian nobles at Wilimow. Still matters went on until 1393 without any resolute attempt to depose him. In that year the citizens of Prague, excited by the order that he had given for the execution of two of their number, and two of the nobles, taking advantage of his visit to a neighbouring monastery with a small retinue, arrested him, and kept him in a dungeon for fifteen weeks. At the end of this time, according to one story, he was allowed, as a special favour, to go and bathe at Old Prague in the Moldau. By the assistance of the girl Susanna, who served at the bath, and who rowed him across the river in a skiff, he escaped, and for some time employed Susanna as his chief adviser, and her likeness is conspicuous among the miniatures of a copy of the Bible which he had illustrated with representations of his captivity. Another account represents him as released at the request of his brother and the other princes of his family. A second captivity, however, awaited him. This time his brother Sigismund and his cousin Jobst of Moravia, with the assistance of the Duke of Austria, seized him, and conveyed him to Vienna. Thence he escaped by the aid of a fisherman who used to bring the prisoner an occasional breakfast for charity's sake. He again, however, shut himself up in his Bohemian castle, and continued his revels.

In 1392 his wife had been killed by one of the hounds that he always had with him; yet, notwithstanding this, and his general loose character and his cruelty, he was able to get another wife, a Bavarian princess, whom he married chiefly to obtain an ally. After this he went on drinking. Germany bore with him, happily seeing little of him for twenty-two years. Bohemia, notwithstanding the strong party made against him by Sigismund and Jobst, had to endure him for nineteen years longer. It may, however, be true that his character has suffered from the patronage, or abstinence from persecution, which he displayed or has the credit of having displayed towards the Hussites. Though there is no evidence to prove that he favoured John Huss, he certainly allowed his teaching in the University of Prague until stopped by the pope. It is barely possible that his vices may have been exaggerated by those who believed him favourable to heresy, but even if that be the case, there is nothing good said of him. He may not have been quite so bad, and yet good for nothing. In Germany his influence was but slightly felt; still the imperial power, although weak, had been so much made of by Charles IV., had been made so conspicuous as to be almost necessary; and the influence of Charles did not pass away all at once, nor was Wenzel without an occasional hazy idea of doing an imperial act. He seems to have had an idea that he ought to interfere in Italy, and sent there occasionally a threatening letter, or appointed an imperial vicar who, like himself, contented himself with promising to interfere, or he issued a commission to settle the claims of the rival popes, or he sanctioned a league, or forbade one, or even himself joined one; but no one seems to have regarded his edicts except so far as they suited his own pleasure, or could be made a pretext for doing something that he wanted to do.

On the death of Urban VI., he recognised and supported Boniface IX.; but, when the Avignon pope, Clement VII, died, he entered into a negotiation with France for the deposition of both the rivals, and even went to Rheims in 1398 to consult on the extirpation of the schism. On this visit it is said that he got so drunk as to acknowledge the wrong pope, Benedict, instead of Boniface, and promised to cede Genoa to the French.

If this is true, it is probably one of the causes that led directly to his deposition. But the most important business of Germany went on with very little interference from him.

In 1381 the cities of Swabia and the Rhine formed themselves into a league against the counts and dukes of Swabia and Bavaria, with Wenzel's sanction. By this league a great part of Bavaria was devastated. But a few years before these same cities had been in strict league with these same nobles. Although it is important to keep before us the political energy exhibited in these alliances, it is almost impossible, however, and quite unnecessary to unravel their short and variable complications.

Switzerland.—In Switzerland the atmosphere is a little clearer. There we find the Austrian dukes, during the long peace that began in 1356, diligently endeavouring to secure and increase their remaining rights. In 1376 they had to encounter Ingelram de Coucy (married Isabella, daughter of Edward III.), who came with a force of Englishmen and Frenchmen to demand the payment of his mother's dowry, Catherine of Austria, which was settled on some of the Swiss towns. Duke Leopold applied for help to the confederate cantons, and Bern and Zürich afforded it. But Coucy's force was very formidable, and caused an immense deal of suffering before it was finally disposed of, partly by battle, partly by starvation.

In 1382 a new quarrel arose. One Count Rudolf attempted to surprise Soleure; he failed, and the Bernese divided his estates with the people of Soleure. This embittered more than ever the relations between the nobles and the towns, and also between Austria and the confederates. This quarrel ended for Leopold at least in the battle of Sempach in 1386, where he was slain in July 1386. His son, Leopold IV., continued the war for a few months, each city grasping at any unprotected territory that lay convenient for it, and the Austrians unable to crush an enemy that seemed ubiquitous. After a year and a half of what was called the Bad Peace, because no one kept it, open war was resumed, but the battle of Naefels, in which a handful of the men of Glarus destroyed a large Austrian force, led to another peace. This was more lasting; it extended from 1388 to 1394, and was afterwards renewed for twenty, and later on, in 1412, for fifty years. But indeed the emancipation of Switzerland from the yoke of Austria was now nearly accomplished. The deliverance of Appenzell from the dominion of the Abbot of St. Gallen was won against the combined force of Austria and the abbot, without disturbing the relations of the confederated cantons; and the Rhœtian or Grison confederations were being created for struggles that were still far in the future.

Deposition of Wenzel. — From this time, then, Switzerland may be regarded, for our present purpose, as lying outside of Germany. But it is time to have done with Wenzel. He was deposed, and the deposition was actually treated as valid, although his successor was only partially recognised. As this is certainly a very exceptional case, and as the circumstances bring out nearly everything that I have not mentioned, that is worth remembering as to the Wenzel's acts, we will run through the particular circumstances of it. Wenzel had long been a shame and grief to Germany, without any one finding or making it his business to get rid of him. In a healthy state of the papacy he must have been excommunicated, and that might have led to deposition, but in this case there was no pope strong enough to exercise jurisdiction in Germany, except the pontiff who owed the maintenance of his position to the support of Wenzel and his allies. It was a case clearly in which the empire must act for itself, and it did so. The three ecclesiastical electors and the two prince electors who, according to the Golden Bull, were entitled to be vicars of the empire during a vacancy, took the initiative. The immediate provocation was the sale of Milan to the Visconti and of Genoa to the French. Genoa made itself over to France in 1396; what Wenzel did at Rheims in 1398 is not clear. In September 1399 they met at Mainz and determined to appoint a single vicar of the empire. Wenzel refused to recognise or appoint him, and the next move was to invite him in person to Frankfort to meet the princes. Wenzel refused to leave Bohemia, and his ambassadors protested against the holding of assemblies of the princes without his sanction. Matters went dragging on for nearly a year. At last with the advice of Boniface IX. the electors met at Lahnstein, and, having waited for ten days for Wenzel to appear, they deposed him on August 24, 1400.

Criticism.—The act or sentence which was pronounced by the Archbishop of Mainz as Arch-chancellor of Germany, declares that Wenzel is the chief author of the abuses prevailing in the empire, and that he has treated the remonstrances of the princes with scandalous contumacy. It then proceeds to state the grounds of accusation; he has sold Genoa to France, and Lombardy to Galeazzo Visconti; he has alienated imperial domain by sale; he has sold blank letters patent, to be filled up by the purchasers at their will; he has granted impunity to thieves and robbers; he has cruelly murdered, drowned, and burned prelates, priests, and nobles; he has made a league with Poland against the Teutonic knights; he has wasted the revenues of the empire of Bohemia, destroyed the University of Prague; given himself up to debauchery and neglected the affairs of the empire. He is therefore deposed and deprived.

A good deal might be said both for and against the exact constitutional character of such an act, but nothing could be said for Wenzel. On the strict letter of the old German institutions, as existing both in England and in Germany, there was in the witenagemot a power of deposing a bad or worthless prince, but it was long since such a thing had been done with any regard to formality. In England, the year before, a precedent had been given; and, bad as Richard's case was, that of Wenzel was worse. For years before it had been the common talk of Europe that such a measure was necessary. Richard II. himself had been persuaded that his good government of England had so impressed the Germans that they were ready to choose him instead of his brother-in-law, Wenzel, and that was regarded as one of the first hallucinations that culminated in his attempt at revolution. But, although the charges made against Richard were very much like those against Wenzel, the part taken by Henry of Lancaster in his deposition takes away from the similarity in its most important point. The deposition of Richard was brought about quite as much by private rivalry as by public indignation; it was the adjudication of the crown that he had thrown away to a claimant who had intrigued to supplant him. Wenzel's was a solemn act of popular or rather national judgment and justice; and it was performed by all the body of the electors except himself and his cousin, Jobst of Moravia, to whom Sigismund, when (in 1386) he became King of Hungary, had mortgaged the margraviate of Brandenburg. The Duke of Saxony, however, was not present at the conference. The final sentence was not issued until all had been prepared for the election of a new king.

As early as May the electors at Rhense had fixed on Duke Frederick of Brunswick, and he, in preparation for the event, had gone into his own dominions to prepare men and money. But whilst thus employed, or when on his way to Lahnstein, he was attacked by the Count of Waldeck and killed in the month of June at Fritzlar. The Duke of Saxony, who was in his company, was wounded, and was thus prevented from taking part in the further proceedings.

Election of Rupert of the Pale. — The place of Frederick as a candidate was supplied by Rupert, the Count Palatine of the Rhine. He undertook to accept the office on the same day that the sentence against Wenzel was promulgated, and also to recover Milan and to undo the other unlawful acts of Wenzel. Rupert was the representative of the older branch of the house of Wittelsbach; his career did not make him an exception to the usual luck of that house when it made a stroke for empire. He is the second of the list that is made up by the Emperor Lewis of Bavaria, Frederick, King of Bohemia, the son-in-law of James I., and the unfortunate Charles VII., who endeavoured in the eighteenth century to supplant the Austrian family and oust the husband of Maria Theresa.

Rupert was a brave and able prince, but the disorganised state in which the empire was when he undertook it might have proved too much for the abilities of a much stronger one. The election at Rhense and Lahnstein was but a short step towards the acquisition of the empire. Wenzel was by no means without partisans, and these were unwilling to accept Rupert until it was clear that Wenzel would do nothing to help himself. Frankfort declined to admit him, and he had to spend six weeks in a siege before he could make himself master of that imperial and capital city. After Frankfort had submitted, Strassburg also received him, but Aix-la-Chapelle hesitated; and ultimately the coronation was performed at Cologne, contrary to precedent and contrary to the Golden Bull. He held, however, his first diet at Nuremberg in proper order in May, and there, after strengthening his position as much as he could by the usual plan of confirming the privileges of all who were willing to adhere to him, he prepared for that Italian expedition to which he had bound himself when he accepted his election as King of the Romans. At the same time he thought it necessary to make some provision in case Wenzel should resist, as he was strongly urged to do by his brother, Sigismund, and cousin, Jobst, both of whom had an idea of their own fitness for the empire.

Resistance, however, was the last thing that Wenzel thought of. He declined to do more than listen to the arguments of France, and he would not do so much as that for Sigismund; but, whilst he was yet speaking to him, left the room and went to his bath. He had the support of Rudolf of Saxony and Ernest of Bavaria, who was jealous of his cousin's exaltation, and that was nearly all: Sigismund and Jobst had rather connived at his deposition, but had no desire for the dismemberment of the family territory. Wenzel, however, cared little for any of them, or even for the siege which he endured in Prague from the Bohemian nobles in league with Rupert's party. Rupert himself seems to have had no wish to drive matters to extremity with either Wenzel or his family.

Matters were, therefore, sufficiently advanced in August 1401 for the new expedition. In September, at Augsburg, Rupert appointed his son Lewis vicar of the empire for Alemannia, Gaul, and the kingdom of Arles, having already made him his representative in Bavaria and the Palatinate. On September 25 he was at Innsbrück, on October 2 at Brixen; at Trent on the 14th. There is a good deal of obscurity both as to the movements and companions of Rupert, and this period is slurred over by historians generally. It seems, however, certain that he had brought with him only a small force, expecting probably that, as had been usual on former expeditions, one section of the Italians would rise in his favour.

Rupert in Italy.—It appears that he expected also succours from England, with which country he had connected himself by a marriage between his son Lewis and Blanche of Lancaster, daughter of Henry IV. He was not, therefore, prepared for so speedy resistance as Gian Galeazzo Visconti had for him. Between October 16 and 21 he advanced into the territory of Brescia, and there the forces of Milan met him. He had with him Duke Leopold of Austria, the Archbishop of Cologne, and a body of Italian cavalry under Jacopo da Carrara. On the 21st a battle was fought, and the result was unfavourable to Rupert. According to Sismondi, he was saved from a downright rout by the Paduan cavalry; but the German historians allow that it was an out and out defeat: he was forced to retire on

Trent; the Duke of Austria and Archbishop of Cologne left him; the English succours had not yet arrived, and the Florentine subsidy, on which he had largely relied for the support of such force as he had, was only partly paid. He seems to have given up the idea of thinking of penetrating to Rome and receiving the imperial crown. Before Christmas he went from Trent to Padua and Venice, attempting, by the aid of the Florentines, and at their request, to draw in the pope and the republic of Venice into a league against the Visconti. But they, seeing him so ill-supported by Germany, drew back. He stayed at Padua until April 1402, and then went back to Germany. The success of Gian Galeazzo seemed secure, and his dream of becoming King of Italy ready to be fulfilled. This result, terrible and shameful for the empire, was averted by the plague. Gian Galeazzo died of it the September after the battle of Brescia. His estates were left in a very unsettled condition, and his powerful rule at Milan was succeeded by anarchy; but Rupert, although urged by both Germans and Florentines, refused to make another attempt on Italy. He showed his wisdom and good faith in devoting himself to the pacification and regulation of those parts of Germany that adhered to him. Rupert was indeed born a brave man and a man of business; the register of his extant acts fills almost as large a volume as that of the acts of Lewis of Bavaria; and as that prince did, he spent the remaining years of his reign in his own territory, chiefly at Heidelberg in the Palatinate, or on the imperial domain at Oppenheim. In this employment he had sufficient work for a long life.

Rupert in Germany.—The first transaction he undertook, after his return from Italy, was to compel Aix-la-Chapelle to recognise him. This was not done until he had put the city under the imperial ban; nor even then until the burghers had formally renounced their allegiance to Wenzel. He next had to put down the Margrave of Baden, who, supported by the Duke of Orleans and the French party, and countenanced by Wenzel, was exercising the unjust customs on the Rhine. The margrave was obliged or persuaded to submit. But similar measures of constraint used against the robber counts of the Wetterau, some of whom were vassals of the Archbishop of Mainz, had the unfortunate result of exasperating that influential and unscrupulous prelate against him.

John of Nassau, the archbishop, had taken a leading part in the deposition of Wenzel, and was not free from the suspicion of having connived at the struggle which caused the death of Frederick of Brunswick. He took, therefore, to himself the credit of having placed Rupert on the throne; and now, finding that Rupert's sense of justice, stronger than his gratitude, would not allow him to spare even the vassals of the archbishop, he placed himself in connection with a league formed against him. This league was based on the Wetterau confederation formed under Wenzel, the head of which was Philip of Nassau, the archbishop's brother: one of those local confederations possessing some claim to a real organisation, which, under Maximilian, a century later, were recognised as, or developed into, the system of circles.

This Wetterau league, with the archbishop, Count Eberhard of Würtemberg, the representative of a long line of petty tyrants, the Margrave of Baden, and forty-seven of the cities of Swabia and Strassburg, under the title of the Confederation of Marbach, wore the unfortunate King of the Romans to death. Summons after summons was issued, to bring the confederates, if possible, before a diet; but on one pretext or another they failed to appear, and the Archbishop of Mainz grew so bold as to send letters of defiance to Rupert. It is not easy to say whether Rupert was quite in the right in all his proceedings against the confederates. The acceptance of Ortenau and Offenbach from the Bishop of Strassburg, as the price of his assistance against the citizens of that town, is alleged against him as degrading the imperial dignity; but that he was a poor man is certain, and sufficient reason for such charges being brought against him by unfavourable historians, just as in his Italian expedition he is treated by Sismondi as a mercenary of Florence. But both his acts and his general reputation show him to have tried how to be a just prince.

The Council of Pisa.—One of Rupert's last public acts was a preparation for the Council of Pisa. His relation to the popes who, in succession, opposition, or combination, were claiming to rule the Church was this: Boniface IX., in 1403, on finding that Wenzel's cause was hopeless, had recognised Rupert as King of the Romans. In 1398 Wenzel and Charles VI., a couple of madmen, as we saw, had agreed to persuade the two popes, Boniface IX. and Benedict XIII., to close the schism by voluntarily resigning. Boniface held out a half-promise that he would do so, but Benedict obstinately declined; his refusal made Charles his enemy, and from 1398 to 1403 he was a prisoner at Avignon. He was, in fact, the victim of the quarrel between Burgundy and Orleans, who could not agree on a consistent or common policy. In 1404 Boniface died, and first Innocent VII., and, two years after, Gregory XII., were elected at Rome; the

latter under promise to resign if the Pope of Avignon
would do so; Benedict still ruling at Avignon. These
Italian popes were recognised by Rupert, as by Germany and England generally, but the scandal was felt
to be a very wretched one; and again the scheme of
a double resignation was propounded; and again it
failed. Each pope summoned a council: Gregory at
Cividale, Benedict at Perpignan.

In 1409 the cardinals summoned the prelates, who
wished for the end of the schism, to meet at Pisa. In
preparation for this assembly, Rupert held a diet at
Nuremberg, and afterwards another at Frankfort. In
these assemblies the majority showed themselves in
favour of the cardinals, but Rupert and a few others
clung to Gregory, who had promised to leave the arbitration to him, and make him "advocate" or "defensor"
of the Roman Church. The council, warned of his
design, refused to receive his representatives, giving
admission instead to those of Wenzel. In April 1409
the Council of Pisa deposed both popes, and elected a
third, Alexander V.; but, as neither Benedict nor Gregory
accepted their decision, the schism was rather increased
than diminished. Rupert continued faithful to Gregory,
but he did not live to see matters further complicated,
as they were by the death of Alexander (May 8, 1410).

Death of Rupert, 1410.—German affairs were becoming very threatening, and, year after year, he
found it more difficult to keep the kingdom in order.
None of the lucky windfalls came to him that had
helped to found the house of Luxemburg, and even
to give a temporary predominance to that of Bavaria.
Worn out with anxiety and toil, he died at Oppenheim
on May 18, 1410, *æt.* fifty-eight, leaving the reputation
of an able and honest prince, whom not even his

poverty could prevent from acting in accordance with his views of right. His last measure, far from securing the aggrandisement of his family, broke up the unity of it for a time and deprived it of any chance of making head against the great territorial princes. This was to direct the division of his dominions among his sons. Lewis, the eldest, held the Electorate, with the territory of Amberg; John held the Upper Palatinate with Neuburg, and founded a branch that fell in in 1448. Stephen had Simmern, and founded a branch which in 1559 succeeded to the Electorate. Otto, the fourth, founded the line of Mosbach, which terminated in 1499.

I mention these things to illustrate the effect of the system of succession which in so many of the great families counteracted all their efforts for the aggregation of estates. Saxony, Bavaria in a less degree, and the Palatinate, by these divisions were absolutely powerless against the houses of Luxemburg and Austria, which adopted it with much more restriction. Their condition led, no doubt, to the consolidation of the empire as an hereditary institution, in the house of Hapsburg, a consummation which, however great were the glories that Charles V. illustrated it with, was quite out of keeping with the long traditional policy of the princes. As long as the electorates were great principalities, as long as they represented in any degree the nations out of which Germany was created, the empire was really as well as nominally elective.

Germany in the Fifteenth Century. — In tracing the history of Sigismund in the next chapter, I shall have to turn back to some of the important events in which he was concerned, which are less connected with the history of Germany but cannot be omitted from it, such as the invasion of Europe by Bajazet, the growth of Hussitism, and the relations of the Sclavonic kingdoms with each other and with Naples. The reigns of Wenzel and Rupert form the very dullest portions of proper German history: absence of important incident, and even of constitutional developments. There is not, indeed, so complete disorganisation as in the middle of the century, but the strength of the organisation that superficially spread over the kingdom, scarcely could hide the disruption and dismemberment going on below the surface, and cannot be regarded as real. It was a thin web of pomp and circumstance woven by Charles IV., and not yet torn to pieces by the wind floating on it by its very lightness. Sigismund was to make more of it. Frederick Maximilian and Charles were to make much more still; but rather by throwing into the medley of interests their own great territorial influence and position in Europe, by strengthening their place in Germany and the imperial name, by their power as dukes of Austria and Burgundy; and, further, by their position as kings of Spain and Naples, Bohemia and Hungary. The empire itself was attenuated, but the imperial crown worn by the King of Bohemia and Hungary, Naples or Spain, the Indies, Sicily, and Jerusalem was very imposing, and by the right of its wearer, a very powerful influence throughout the world.

IMPORTANT DATES

Wenzel, 1378–1400.
League of German Towns, 1381.
Battle of Sempach, 1386.
Battle of Naefels, 1388.
The Union of Kalmar, 1397.
Deposition of Wenzel, 1399.
Rupert of the Palatinate Emperor, 1400–1410.
Council of Pisa, 1409.
Battle of Tannenberg, 1410.

L

CHAPTER IX

The disputed succession—Election of Sigismund—His previous history—The great schism—The Council of Constance—John Huss—Sigismund in France and England—Election of Martin V.—The Bohemian War—The Council of Basel—Sigismund's death, 1437—The situation in Germany—Accession of Albert of Austria—His acts—His death, 1439.

Sigismund Emperor. — The death of King Rupert took place on May 18, 1410. According to the Golden Bull it was the duty of the Archbishop of Mainz, within a month of the vacancy, to summon the electors to Frankfort, and the electors were to meet within three months, to spend not more than a month in the business. In strict conformity with this rule, John of Nassau, the archbishop, who had made himself so strong an opponent of Rupert, summoned the electors for September 1, and, on that day, the three archbishops and the Count Palatine, Lewis, son of the late king, were present. Wenzel, of course, having never allowed the election of Rupert, did not recognise the vacancy, although he must have allowed his ambassador to appear in the diet: Rudolf of Saxony was employed in a war on the Polish border in defence of the cross-bearing knights of Livonia, and Jobst of Moravia, the mortgagee, as well as Sigismund of Hungary, the mortgagor, of the electorate of Brandenburg, were present by ambassadors. The ambassador of Sigismund was Frederick, burgrave of Nuremberg, Prince of Hohenzollern. Sigismund was the most prominent candidate; indeed, although it was known that

Jobst would like to be elected, and was a man of mature age and sound habits of business, Sigismund was the only person who showed much anxiety about it; he had already obtained the support of Pope Gregory XII. and of the Elector Palatine. The Archbishop of Mainz begged for delay in order that the Duke of Saxony, at least, might be present; but the burgrave, Frederick, would not consent, and the result was a double or disputed election; the Elector Palatine, the Archbishop of Trèves, and Frederick as representing Sigismund, elected him on September 20; the Archbishop of Mainz and Cologne, with the ambassadors of Jobst, Wenzel, and Saxony, elected Jobst himself on October 1.

Notwithstanding the disputed right to Brandenburg and the questionable credentials of Wenzel's representatives, Jobst had a clear majority, and was duly elected on October 1. But it does not appear that he ever was crowned, and he died in little more than three months, on January 8, leaving not only Brandenburg but the imperial crown free for Sigismund. This time there was no opposition; Sigismund was elected, after some little delay, on July 21, 1411. Sigismund stands before the world, for so long a time and in so many capacities, that he occupies more room in history than the length or importance of his reign as King of the Romans and emperor deserves; but as it is almost impossible to estimate the latter without some reference to the earlier adventures of this adventurous prince, we must look back to the two last reigns and even farther.

Sigismund was the son of Charles IV., and, as Wenzel had no children, he is throughout his brother's life heir-presumptive to the kingdom of Bohemia and to the other possessions of the Luxemburg house. In 1373 his father had bestowed upon him the march of Brandenburg, and in his youth he was married to Mary, the daughter of Lewis the Great, King of Poland and Hungary, who intended to make him his heir in both those kingdoms. This king Lewis was a descendant of the first house of Anjou established in Naples; his father was Carobert, King of Hungary, son of Charles Martel, son of Charles II. of Naples by the heiress of the Hungarian line.

Sigismund's Relations with Naples, Hungary, Poland.—In Naples, as you may remember, Charles Martel, having died before his father, Robert, the antagonist of Henry of Luxemburg and patron of John XXII., had succeeded to the prejudice of Carobert; and, as in both Naples and Hungary, there were at the same time two or three rival kings or claimants, the complication of the two successions is very puzzling. Lewis of Hungary had, however, been elected King of Poland on the death of his maternal uncle in 1370; and, although he persistently interfered in the affairs of Naples, is not counted among the kings. On the death of Lewis, however, in 1382, Sigismund put in his claims for both crowns of Poland and Hungary.

Lewis had, by great concessions to the Polish nobles, obtained their promise to elect him to that elective crown: in Hungary he trusted to his own popularity and the established doctrine of hereditary succession. Sigismund found, however, that his claims were controverted in both kingdoms. The Poles, forgetful of their word, preferred Hedwiga the younger to Mary the elder daughter of Lewis, refused to have anything to say to Sigismund, and, after an interregnum of four years, made up a marriage between Hedwiga and Jagello, Duke of Lithuania, in consequence of which he was to receive Christianity and succeed to the kingdom.

Poor Hedwiga, who was engaged to William of Austria, was the victim of policy, and led an unhappy life with a disagreeable, half-heathen husband; but so Sigismund lost Poland. In Hungary he succeeded better, but not without a struggle. There, as you may remember, Charles of Durazzo, having murdered the Queen of Naples and got possession of that throne, arrived in Hungary in 1385 to take advantage of the female succession there, and was murdered by order of Elizabeth, the widow of King Lewis and mother of the young queen Mary. Elizabeth herself was soon after taken and drowned by the Ban of Croatia, a partisan of Charles, and at last Sigismund appeared, rescued his bride, and completed his marriage in 1386. The heir of Naples was Ladislaus, son of Charles of Durazzo, and adversary of Pope John XXIII. Sigismund, when fairly seated in Hungary, mortgaged his electorate of Brandenburg to his cousin, Jobst of Moravia, great-grandson, like himself, of Henry VII. From this time he reigned in Hungary without dispute until 1392, but not without difficulty and danger; for his severity is said to have provoked the Hungarian nobles against him; he was obliged to be constantly on the watch against the Wallachians, who were being forced on to Hungary by the advances of the Turks, and he had his brother Wenzel to keep in view, lest, in some mad freak, he should make away with the Bohemian inheritance; as we saw, he had at one time to be a party to his imprisonment, and was a consenting one, although with some reluctance and perhaps no little feeling of disappointment, to his deposition from the German throne.

In 1392, just as Sigismund had won some successes

in Bulgaria over the Turks and Wallachians, he heard of his wife's death and had to return to Hungary to counteract the machinations of Jagello, now called Ladislas or Uladislas, who was claiming the crown as the husband of Hedwiga. Setting himself in earnest to secure his hold on the kingdom, he seemed likely to succeed, but the constant attacks of the Wallachians gave him little breathing time. In this difficulty he summoned crusaders from all the west of Europe to his aid. They came, and perished mostly in the great battle of Nicopolis, September 28, 1396, which made Sigismund a fugitive and wanderer for a year and a half. When he appeared again in Hungary he was seized by the discontented nobles and imprisoned. The crown was offered by the same party to the other Ladislaus, the one of Naples, and accepted by him. He was crowned in 1403 ; but, a few days after the coronation, Sigismund escaped from prison, hastened to Bohemia, and there collected force enough from Wenzel's subjects to drive Ladislaus back to Naples. The nobleman by whose assistance this was done, the Count of Cilly, lent him his aid on condition that he married his daughter Barbara. This Sigismund did, and they led a very unhappy life together for more than thirty years. It is just, however, to poor Barbara to say that, although the Catholic writers give her a bad character, the Hussites showed some regard and respect for her, and it is possible that the charges of atheism and the likeness to Messalina, alleged against her, are exaggerations.

The Schism. — From the time of his escape and recovery of Hungary Sigismund seems to have reigned in peace until the death of Rupert, when his ambition for the imperial crown was raised, and after the death of Jobst gratified. From the time of his election, 1412, to his death, 1437, he was the most prominent man in Europe. The first and greatest of his undertakings was the peace of the Church, the putting an end to the schism. In this he clearly acted both with sincerity and with a real sense of his responsibility as King of the Romans. In 1410, just before the death of King Rupert, John XXIII. (Balthazar Cossa) had been chosen by the cardinals at Bologna to succeed their pope, Alexander V.; Benedict XIII. and Gregory XII. still, although deposed by the Council of Pisa, claiming and exerting the rights of supreme pontiffs.

One of the first acts of John was to summon (August 15, 1411) and excommunicate King Ladislaus of Naples (1386 to 1414); a measure which, coupled with his summary defeat by Ladislaus, had the effect of throwing the pope into close alliance with Sigismund, and as a general council was Sigismund's remedy for the schism, the pope had to consent. In the year 1413 it was summoned to meet at Constance. One of the great subjects of deliberation in this council was the suppression of the Hussite movement, a measure most important to Sigismund, if the Bohemian crown, so long endangered by the behaviour of Wenzel, were to continue in his family.

The Council of Constance, 1414.—The council opened on October 1, 1414. Sigismund, before he presented himself in person at Constance, was crowned at Aix-la-Chapelle, November 8, 1414, and appeared in the council on Christmas Day (December 25), when he officiated as deacon at the morning Mass.

With the business of the council we cannot deal, except so far as its results touch German history and illustrate the character and position of Sigismund. The surrender of John Huss (arrested November 28, before Sigismund arrived), who had come to the council on the strength of the royal word, is a blot on the character of Sigismund, notwithstanding the equitable considerations that may be alleged in excuse, and will in all probability never be effaced. Sigismund had given the safe-conduct; the pope and cardinals insisted on the imprisonment of the accused. For three months Sigismund resisted, but at last allowed himself to be overborne.

To us neither the loose morality of the age nor the convenient prevalence of the doctrine that no faith is to be kept with heretics, can be allowed to justify even if it be suffered to extenuate the guilt of the act. It cannot be denied that the moral sense, even of that age, was offended, and the verdict of all posterity condemns the betrayal. But we must consider what Sigismund had at stake; how great was the object for which he thought the sin to be necessary. He was determined to put down the schism in the papacy; and this was the price that he had to pay to win the support of the council. By dint of great pressure John XXIII. was made, in March 1415, to consent to abdicate; but the consent was evaded as soon as it was made; and on March 25 he escaped in disguise from the council under the protection of Duke Frederick of Austria, a great enemy of Sigismund, who had compelled him to do homage for his fiefs, and with the connivance of the intriguing Archbishop of Mainz, John of Nassau.

Journey of Sigismund, 1415-1417.—The council, in conjunction with Sigismund, executed summary vengeance on the duke; he was put to the ban of the empire, excommunicated, all his vassals were released from their fealty, and within a month he was compelled to put himself at the king's mercy. The pope, having ruined his protector, was obliged, a month later, to surrender. He was arrested by Frederick of Hohenzollern, burgrave of Nuremberg, and imprisoned. On May 29 he was deposed from the papacy. Gregory XII. abdicated early in July. The same month (July 6, 1415) John Huss was burned. Only one pope now remained in the field, Benedict XIII., and him the council in vain attempted to circumvent. On July 21 Sigismund left the council, under the protection of the Count Palatine; and, as in former days popes preached crusades, he undertook a long journey in person to bring the kings of Europe to a proper sense of the need of peace in the Church. Partly by way of raising funds for his journey he sold the electorate of Brandenburg to Frederick of Hohenzollern, and invested him with it in the council (he had investiture April 18, 1417); thus giving to the indefatigable house, from which the kings of Prussia spring, their second or rather third step on the ladder of empire. Sigismund proceeded first to Basel and thence to Narbonne and Perpignan. His efforts in this direction were successful; he obtained the adhesion of Aragon, Castille, and Navarre to the council, although he could not get Pope Benedict to resign.

From Catalonia he went to Lyons, where the French government entreated him to mediate for Charles VI. with Henry V. of England, who had just won the battle of Agincourt. Coming to Paris on March 1, 1416, he was received with some share of the respect due of old to the imperial dignity. There, one day, as he was attending the court of law, he managed, by conferring knighthood on one of the petitioners to the parliament of Paris, in order to put him on a level with his adversary, to offend the dignity of the great nation; and use was made of this piece of carelessness, by the party indisposed to peace, to reject his overtures. He therefore went on to England, whither Henry V. had invited him to deliberate on measures calculated to put down the heresy that was springing up in their respective dominions. He was not, however, allowed to land at Dover without giving a promise that he would attempt no act of imperial dignity in this island, as he had just done at Paris. Sigismund made no objection, landed on April 30, 1416, and at Southwark was met by the king himself. His visit was one long scene of festivity and triumph; but his mediation for peace failed here as well as at Paris, and an alliance, offensive and defensive, with Henry, which produced no practical result, was all that came of the visit.

After spending nearly four months in England, on August 24 he sailed away, having spent most of his money and with difficulty got ships to take him up the Rhine; he reached Aix-la-Chapelle at last, and went on thence to Constance, where he found the council waiting for him, in January 1417. His exertions on behalf of the council had been more favoured than his attempts to mediate between England and France. The adhesion of Spain had added a fifth nation to the other four—Italy, Germany, France, and England. Immediately Benedict XIII. was summoned; not appearing, he was declared contumacious, and on July 20 deposed as a schismatic. On November 8 Otto Colonna was elected as Pope Martin V.

Election of Martin V., 1417.—The Council of Constance is prominent in ecclesiastical history for something more than the burning of John Huss and conclusion of the great schism; I mean, of course, its attempt, renewed at the Council of Basel some years later, to set its authority as a general council above the authority of the pope. All the good men of Europe were anxious for a reformation of Church discipline, and for the abolition of existing scandals such as those by which the court of Rome was immemorially supported. The appointment of a pope was necessary for such a reformation, but experience had shown that no pope hitherto had had both will and power to effect it.

Before proceeding to the election of Martin, the council had bound itself not to separate until the new pope had granted, or taken the initiative in, this most necessary process. From the first act of Martin V. it was seen that he intended no pressure of the council to affect him; he confirmed all the abuses which had been legalised by John XXIII. He wore out the patience of the members of the council by arguing every point that was submitted to him for change. He broke up the concentrated action of the five nations by entering into negotiations with each for a separate measure; and, in the end, got rid of his troublesome advisers without a scandal. The Council broke up on April 22, 1418. Martin V. was more than a match for his electors; he had a policy of his own, to turn the Church into an absolute despotism, which was to reside in the pope. It was contradictory to the very principle that lies at the foundation of the conciliar constitution; he pressed it with the power and prestige of an honest and virtuous pope, and his success ended in the Reformation of the sixteenth century, which might never have been needed if the Council of Constance had had strength enough to carry out its own determination.

The Hussite War.—The Hussite business concerns Germany only indirectly. The heretical party was national, Bohemian, Czech, in contradistinction to the oppressive German orthodoxy. Nor, although for more than a century movements had been going in Germany in the direction of a doctrinal change, was it, for a century to come, time for a really German reformation.

The year after the Council of Constance broke up Sigismund succeeded to the crown of Bohemia. Wenzel died of apoplexy, and left his brother to reap his wild oats. The judicial murder of John Huss and Jerome of Prague had excited the national feeling beyond endurance. John Ziska, a one-eyed Hussite nobleman, undertook the leadership. The Hussite war occupied Sigismund for the next fourteen years. Great cruelties were committed, no doubt, on both sides. Ziska died in 1424, and after his death the party seems to have been less united. But it was always strong enough to tax the whole power of Sigismund, who even ran the risk of losing Hungary from the same cause. In vain a crusade was published against the heretics; they defeated the foreign crusaders as well as the Germans. Cardinal Beaufort, the great-uncle of Henry VI. of England, spent his treasure in the equipment of an army which he was scarcely able to rescue from ignominious defeat. At last, in 1431, the rebellious Bohemians invaded Germany, laid waste their Austrian, Bavarian, and Saxon neighbours; and then a fifth crusade, under Cardinal Julian Cesarini, was completely defeated by them at Taas in August. This hurried sketch brings this section of the story up to the meeting of the Council of Basel.

In this long struggle with his people Sigismund was not heartily supported by Germany, never very plentiful of money or disposed to war except within her own borders. After the publication of the Crusade, which made it a religious war, he was better helped, and still more so when the Hussites began to act on the offensive and attacked Germany. But it may be questioned whether, in the long run, Bohemia would not have rejected both the yoke of Rome and the rule of the Luxemburg family, had not the national party itself been divided, and the Hussites, as the weaker, gone to the wall. During the interval between the councils of Constance and Basel we hear little of Sigismund, or of Germany either, except in connection with Bohemia. But some few changes of importance were taking place. In 1423 the Ballenstadt line, which had ended in Brandenburg exactly 100 years before, came to an end in electoral Saxony. It continued, indeed, to exist in the lines of Lauenburg, and still continues in Anhalt, but these were not strong enough to press their claims against the king, anxious to lay hold on Saxony as an imperial fief; and the strong neighbour, already Margrave of Meissen and Landgrave of Thuringia, who was eager to purchase it. Frederick the Warlike of Meissen, the descendant of the family which had inherited Thuringia from Henry Raspo, outbid the other candidates, and partly in consideration of his money, partly in reward of his support against the Hussites, Sigismund invested him with the electorate in 1425. From him the present royal and ducal houses of Saxony spring.

In 1422 Sigismund married his only daughter Elizabeth to Albert, Duke of Austria, thus for the time consolidating the interest of the two houses, which had hitherto been either enemies or rivals to one another. Of the many promotions of counts into dukes, and the honorary imperial dignities, bestowed in the Netherlands, in Lombardy, and in Germany, by Sigismund on the plan of his father, there is hardly one which affects the balance of power in Germany or the distinct interests which we have traced hitherto, or which have as yet foreshadowed their later greatness.

Council of Basel, 1413.—In 1431, on February 20, died Pope Martin V. The cardinals, whom he had kept under his control, breathed again and revived the project of reformation which he had nipped in the bud. One direction of the Council of Constance was that a council should be held every five years; in 1423 one had met at Pavia, and was transferred to Sienna, but it was very scantily attended, and was prorogued by Martin for seven years, at the expiration of which it was to meet at Basel. It met at Basel, and was opened on July 1, 1431.

Eugenius IV., who had been elected to succeed Martin, had to fight for his Roman territories, and chose to treat the Council of Basel at first with contempt and afterwards with hostility. He would not go to Basel over the Alps; he would not sanction any terms, such as the council was likely to make with the Hussites or with the Greek Church; he would have a separate council of his own, and he summoned it to meet at Bologna. The Council of Basel met for deliberation in December 1431, under that cardinal, Julian Cesarini, who had been so sorely beaten by the Hussites at Taas. He was most urgent for reformation. All Germany was crying aloud for it. There was war between bishops and people in the episcopal dominions, and in the imperial cities. Sigismund was fully alive to the critical nature of the situation; for Bohemia must be saved, whatever else was lost. This was a time for every nerve to be strained, every advantage to be seized. He determined to demand the imperial crown. First, however, he was crowned at Milan with the iron crown of Lombardy; in July he moved on to Sienna, and there stayed, negotiating with the pope for eight months.

The Council of Basel was legislating in spite of the pope; the pope endeavouring to compel Sigismund to break up the council before he would crown him; Sigismund exhausting the patience and the funds of his few Italian friends.

Last Years of Sigismund's Reign.—At last, May 30, 1433, the emperor was crowned, and enabled to return to Basel as Cæsar and Augustus. The pope was obliged to yield so far as to recognise the council as ecumenical. Sigismund stayed, and took part in its proceedings until April 1434. In the autumn of 1433 the legates of the council had made peace in Bohemia by allowing the use of the cup in the Eucharist to the laity. The measure broke up the union between the stricter Hussites and the Calixtines or more moderate party. The three remaining years of Sigismund's life were spent in running up and down Germany and Bohemia, in hopes of peace. The two Bohemian parties, after a bloody struggle, agreed in 1435 that Sigismund should still be king, but should be compelled to have Hussite priests at court, and to treat the new religion on the same footing as the old. But the old emperor, having once got possession of Prague, showed no respect to the compact. His restrictive measures produced another rising, which was effectively crushed. But the nobles were desirous of a stronger government. The wicked Empress Barbara conspired with them and with the Hussites to procure the succession of the King of Poland, to the exclusion of the emperor's son-in-law. Sigismund pacified the nobles by concessions, but he felt that his end was approaching, and finally left Bohemia for Moravia, to take leave of his daughter at Znaim; there, on December 9, 1437, he died at the age of seventy, having nominated his successor, His wife, Barbara, remained in prison until her death.

It appears that she intended to marry the King of Poland, who, as the wicked old woman had been Sigismund's wife for nearly thirty years, may be thought to have had a lucky escape. There was a suspicion of poison, but there was also, as it would appear, a good deal of natural disease, which would account for Sigismund's death. He had been a very busy man all his life, had undergone great hardships, and indulged in many excesses; he was well-nigh broken with the humiliation and disappointment of the last few years, and, considering that his years at the time of his death were greater in number than those of any king who had reigned since Rudolf of Hapsburg, it may be accounted for without poison. We may say of him, I think, that he lived more laboriously than gloriously, and, notwithstanding his great position and wide influence, laboured in the main with little success. His character was not that of a great king, nor was he morally a good man, but his instincts as a ruler were not wholly selfish, nor is he to be judged by a standard higher than that of the age in which he lived.

As to his struggle with the Hussites and other religious parties in Bohemia, it is not difficult to view them dispassionately; for, on the one hand, we have no sympathy with religious persecution, nor do we think that cold-blooded murder is justified by the faith of the murderer, be he Catholic or Protestant. In these disputes we see the same cruelty on both sides, and on neither any show of ordinary good faith; nor were these wars merely religious. I doubt if there ever were a really religious war fought by sincere men only. It was a war between Czech and Teuton, between Bohemian and German, and between nobles and people.

Sigismund and John Huss.—The bad faith of Sigismund to John Huss I do not think can be excused by any special pleading, nor probably would he himself have excused it. It was a breach of German honour as well as of Christian faith. Only remember the great temptation, the certainty that, unless the snake were scotched, Bohemia and probably Hungary, was lost to him; the certainty that, unless he could make terms with the council, it would be impossible to settle the schism, which was gradually destroying both the influence of the Church, the Christian faith, and the possibility of a general peace in Europe; the certainty that he would lose both the practical benefit of a peace, and, what was almost equally dear to him, the glory of having been the man to make it. He was in a great strait, and he chose the greater evil rather than the less. But, as so often happens when men, either kings or subjects, do this, he lost both the good things that he was trying for. He lived to see the Church embroiled again in a dispute, which only failed to become a schism because the principle that he had set himself to support utterly broke down; he died in the midst of the confusion of the later proceedings at Basel. He lost the affections of the Bohemians and Hungarians, and won no glory as emperor. He lived and died a disappointed man, but he had not depth of character to be greatly impressed by disappointment; his buoyancy itself saved him from being utterly unsuccessful. He retained all the dominions that he had accumulated, as long as he lived, and conveyed them on to his son-in-law, a great thing to be said for a German prince in those days.

M

The Empire at Sigismund's Death.—At his death he possessed, besides the remains of imperial territory scattered about Germany and Italy, and the contingent right to the fiefs as they fell in, the kingdoms of Bohemia, which he inherited from his brother, and Hungary, the portion of his first wife, Moravia, which came to him from his cousin Jobst, and Lausitz or Lusatia, which he had from his younger brother John. Luxemburg had been alienated, and, by a marriage of the sister of Jobst with Antony of Burgundy, Duke of Brabant, had fallen to another family, from which the reclamations of Albert, Sigismund's successor, failed to recover it, and from which it ultimately came to the dukes of Burgundy, and through them to the imperial house once more. Sigismund, having but one daughter, and her well provided for, and being himself always poor, made no attempt to add either of the two electorates which escheated during his reign to his hereditary or acquired dominions.

Thus two of the present governing powers of Germany look to him as the author of their independence, Saxony and Prussia, in neither of which has the male line failed since he gave them their electoral crowns. The house of Hohenzollern we have carefully kept in view from its first rise under Frederick Barbarossa, as counts of Zollern, as burgraves of Nuremberg, as princes of the empire, now as electors of Brandenburg. The house of Saxony we have also traced as first counts Palatine of Saxony, counts of Wettin, then landgraves of Thuringia, and margraves of Meissen, at last dukes and electors.

With these exceptions the face of Germany had not changed much under Sigismund's government. Austria, Bavaria, and the counts and cities of Swabia divided the south. The Count Palatine and the electoral territories

of Mainz and Cologne ruled along the Rhine and in
Westphalia. In the country which was formerly Lower
Saxony were the houses of Brunswick, Saxony, and
Brandenburg, the two former and sometimes the latter
wasting their influence by constant subdivision of territories; beyond were the free cities of the Hanse league,
to the north and to the east the dukes of Mecklenburg
and Pomerania, and then the territories of the Teutonic
knights.

The Hapsburgs.—The house of Austria was the largest
territorial holder in Germany itself; for of the Luxemburg
heritage, a great part lay outside Germany proper, and
was inhabited by Slavonians. And the Austrian dukes
had managed their property well, keeping it together,
under the joint administration of brothers, so as to avoid
dismemberment; only in 1411, a family quarrel ended in
the separation of the duchy of Austria from those of the
Tyrol and Carinthia. Austria fell to Albert, the son-in-
law, at a later date, of Sigismund; Carinthia, Styria, and
Carniola to Ernest, his cousin, father of Frederick III.,
who afterwards became emperor; Tyrol, with the remainder of the Hapsburg inheritance in Alsace, to that
Frederick whom we saw put to the ban of the empire
at the Council of Constance. Thus at the time of the
death of Sigismund there were three dukes of Austria;
and, all through the early part of the century, when the
empire went begging, there was no Austrian duke strong
enough to enter into competition for it; they went on,
however, accumulating territory by happy marriages
and biding their time. The whole dominion, with all
its additions, ultimately centred in Maximilian, and not
before.

The Emperor Albert, 1438–1439.—The death of Sigismund was the event that lodged the empire for the

remaining centuries of its existence (with the exception of the years 1742–1744) in the hands of the Hapsburgs. He had nominated his son-in-law, Duke Albert of Lower Austria, to be King of Bohemia and Hungary after his death—a man of forty-four, of sturdy, rather rigid German character, a patron of learning, and, like most of the princes of his house, a religious and moral man. He had married Elizabeth of Luxemburg in 1422, receiving with her the march of Moravia, and had signalised himself during his father-in-law's reign by his successes against the Hussites. He obtained speedy recognition in both the kingdoms, was crowned King of Hungary on New Year's Day 1438, and elected King of Bohemia on May 6; after some initial difficulties he was crowned at Prague in July. His election as King of the Romans (March 20, 1438) was managed without any obstacle except from himself. He had promised the Hungarian nobles not to accept the empire without their consent. Hungary, as they thought, had been neglected by Sigismund for his imperial possessions and claims, and had suffered thereby from the Wallachians and Turks. The request was made, on behalf of Albert, by his cousin Frederick of Styria, and, after a good deal of discussion, leave was granted him to become King of the Romans. He then allowed himself to accept the election, and was crowned at Aix-la-Chapelle on May 30.

He held, on July 25, his first diet at Nuremberg. In this assembly he enacted some very important laws, which were the basis of the polity subsequently developed by Maximilian. The first and most important of them was the putting an end to all the feuds that at present existed in Germany in consequence of the *jus diffidationis*, or right of private war. For the decision of such quarrels he appointed a tribunal of *Austregas* or arbitrators, similar to that which Frederick II. had attempted to establish in his *Mainzerrecht* or law of Mainz in 1235. On the plan of this tribunal of appeal Maximilian afterwards erected the Imperial Chamber. The second measure of Albert was to divide Germany, with the exception of Bohemia and Austria, into four circles, those of (1) Bavaria and Franconia; (2) the Rhine and Alsace; (3) Westphalia and the Belgian Provinces; and (4) Saxony. These circles, the internal administration of which was directed to the maintenance of peace, were based possibly on those alliances or confederations for the same purpose which have been mentioned as one of the characteristic features of the later years of the fourteenth century. This plan also was enlarged and adopted throughout the whole empire by Maximilian. Executors of peace were appointed for each circle. In a second diet at Nuremberg Albert increased the number to six, as was the arrangement by Maximilian.

The reign of Albert was marked in Italy by a succession of important councils, in which his constant employment in Germany, and the alarms of a Turkish war, did not suffer him to take much part, and the results of which we shall have to examine, rather than their details, in the ensuing reign. After a doubtful campaign in Hungary, where a doubt of success was equivalent to a defeat, he died on October 27, 1439, at a village called Langendorf, between Vienna and Gran. He was unquestionably a prince of very superior abilities, and might have raised the empire far higher than it had been raised since the days of Henry of Luxemburg, but he was able to show little more than promise. He did not even live to see out the Council of Basel. He died childless, but his wife three months after his death presented Hungary and Bohemia with an hereditary and legitimate sovereign. Germany had to provide one for herself.

IMPORTANT DATES

Sigismund, 1411–1437.
The Council of Constance, 1414–1417.
John Huss is burnt, 1415.
Martin V. Pope, 1417.
Hussite War, 1419–1436.
Council of Basel, 1431.
Albert of Austria Emperor, 1438–1439.

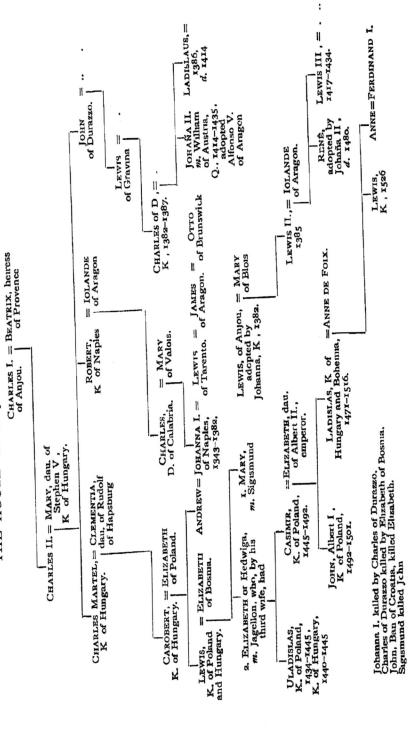

THE HOUSE OF ANJOU IN HUNGARY AND NAPLES

CHARLES I. = BEATRIX, heiress
K of Anjou. | of Provence

Johanna I. killed by Charles of Durazzo.
Charles of Durazzo killed by Elizabeth of Bosnia.
John, Ban of Croatia, killed Elizabeth.
Sigismund killed John

CHAPTER X

The reign of Frederick III.—An epoch in the history of Germany and of the Hapsburgs—The discovery of printing— Frederick's character—Close of the Council of Basel—Wars in Germany, 1440-1452—Bohemia and Hungary—Matthias Corvinus—The Turkish invasions—Death of Filippo Maria Visconti, 1447— John Hunyadi—Death of Albert of Austria, 1463—Results of Frederick's reign—His son Maximilian.

The Reign of Frederick III.—The reign of Frederick III. is the longest and the dullest of all German history. No doubt the fifty-three years of it contained their proper number of facts and events, and some progress of society was made during it ; but the general features are slightly marked, and the philosophy of history has very little to say about it ; even that little is inconsistent with itself ; like the dark ages to the philosophic mind it is obscure, as much because of the obscurity of the philosophic mind as because of its own. Yet the unphilosophic mind cannot descry anything of lasting interest, and the most careful inspection can reveal only a few things that are worth remembering.

As an epoch, however, there can be no doubt that the reign has an importance of its own. In the first place it marks the permanent acquisition, by the house of Hapsburg, of the name and remains of empire. Albert II. left only a posthumous child, who himself had no issue ; from Frederick III. proceeded the whole of the remaining Hapsburg emperors ; and the house, so long as it subsisted in the male line, retained the empire with but a rare and weak attempt on the part of any rival family

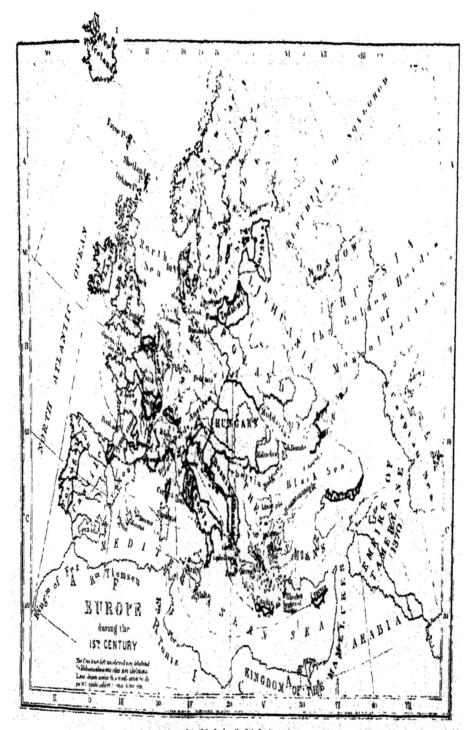

EUROPE
during the
15ᵀᴴ CENTURY

at interruption.   Again Frederick III. was the last
emperor of the Romans who received the imperial
crown in the imperial city. All the succeeding emperors
were not, strictly speaking, more than emperors elect,
except Charles V., who was crowned, however, not at
Rome, but at Bologna. Again by a singular coincidence
the last crowned emperor was the first of the German
line who possessed the imperial title without a counter-
part or equal; for during Frederick's reign, as you will
remember, the Byzantine succession ceased both at
Constantinople and at Trebizond, both cities being taken
by the Turks, and the houses of Palæologus and Com-
nenus alike ceasing to claim even the heritage of the
Cæsarship. The fall of the Byzantine empire, and the
permanent settlement of the Turks in Europe, is enough
to mark, as an epoch, the reign of the principal sovereign
of Europe under whom it occurred. It placed in permanent and irreconcilable opposition the house of
Austria and the Turkish empire, whose struggles for the
sovereignty of Eastern Europe, after lasting spasmodically for three centuries, may possibly be determined
in the fourth; at all events from this dates the assumption by the Austrian house of the defence of European
Christendom on the eastern frontier, a defence character-
ised by many hard-fought battles, and brilliant victories,
and narrow escapes.

Another great event is that of the discovery of printing, all the probable dates of which fall within the half
century of Frederick's reign. Outside the empire, or on
the borders of it, there are abundant interesting and
important phenomena; the growth of the house of
Burgundy, the corresponding growth of the real power
of the French Monarchy under Lewis XI.—in England
both the Wars of the Roses, and the pacification and

development that followed from it. In Spain the union
of Aragon and Castille, and the conquest of the Moors;
the consolidation of the several powers, whose struggles
and the balance of whose power makes up modern
history. In many countries the step from medieval to
modern is itself taken, whilst Frederick III. is sole and
last crowned Cæsar. The great struggle between the
papal and conciliar systems of Church government is
settled at least for the Roman portion of the Church
during the same period.

Yet Germany has little or no history. Is it difficult to
say why? There were wars enough. All South Germany
seems to have been in a chronic state of private war;
there were wars with the Turks on the frontier; and in
Hungary and Bohemia wars of nationality and religion;
on the western boundary there were wars of conquest
and wars of liberation; and something of the same sort
on the north in the Netherland cities, and the struggles
of Burgundy for supremacy there. There were wars in
Prussia, internal and external; wars in Switzerland and
Italy; but there was no imperial war. Frederick was
able, for the most part, to live at Vienna or Neustadt,
gardening by day and star-gazing by night, whilst the
old things, all round him, were rapidly passing away, and
the old order giving place to the new. He himself, in
dignity and in some sort in worth also, the first of the
players, has the least share and the least interest in the
game. It may be that he has also the least stake in it;
yet he plays, as it were, with a view to the future of his
house. His magnificent dreams and imperial devices
suit well enough with the fortunes of his posterity. His
device of A.E.I.O U., *Austriæ est imperare orbi universo,*
would read but as the veriest dotage of effete imperialism,
were it not that we see it so nearly fulfilled in the grand,

almost unbounded empire of his great-grandson, Charles V., that one might almost think that his astrology had taught him truer lessons than are divined by the political foresight of most men. Small indeed were the attempts he made to increase either the power or the territory of his own house. And this is his strong point. He was very honest, and, if ambitious at all, only so within the limits of just dealing. His imperial authority was little more than a shadow; but that little of it, which was substantial, was used righteously. He had little territory, but that little he did his best to keep in peace.

It is absurd, with some modern historians, to blame him for having lowered the status of the empire. He may be blamable for accepting the dignity, but, having accepted it, he could but use it according to the power that he had before. Albert, Sigismund, Wenzel, Charles IV., had had what share of power they had had in Europe and in Germany, under the title indeed of empire, but by virtue of their hereditary estates, inside and outside of Germany; the Luxemburgs, by their Bohemian and Hungarian possessions, and Albert in the right of his Luxemburg wife.

Frederick is accused of having lost hold of the Luxemburg heritages; but in truth he never had hold of them, nor could have seized them, except by a breach of trust that would have been revolting to him, or by an act of tyranny for which he had perhaps no will, and certainly no power. Since Lewis of Bavaria and Rupert there had been no emperor with so little hereditary power, and Lewis had put an end to what little remained of imperial power in the body of Germany. Frederick had the opportunity of increasing his family strength by the marriage of his children, and Maximilian, by his marriage, did lay the foundation of the strength, as a European power, of the house of Hapsburg. He built on the heritage of his Burgundian wife, as John of Bohemia had on the inheritance of his Bohemian wife; and as Albert of Austria had on Elizabeth of Luxemburg. But Frederick surely cannot be charged with losing what he never had. The kingdoms of Albert descended to his posthumous son Ladislas. Frederick refused them, when they were offered to him, because he would not infringe the rights of his ward; and when Ladislas died in 1457, Frederick was not strong enough to claim them, either as heir or as emperor, or by virtue of family compacts, as an inheritance, or an escheat. His weakness is thus accounted for, and accounts for much more. He was very far from being a great prince, but not so far from being a good one; and might no doubt have been much greater if he had been less good. But in the Middle Ages good princes are too scarce to be worthy of ridicule and contempt; and honesty and integrity are not the less virtues when they are possessed by a man too weak to struggle, but not too weak to lie and cheat, if he had chosen. The reign has no plot or dramatic unity like some of the shorter ones. Frederick's character and proceedings do not make him the nucleus of any great set of incidents. The world went on around him very much as if he were not there.

Albert II. left his wife, the last representative of the house of Luxemburg, near her confinement. Frederick, Duke of Styria, the nearest of his agnates, was in a family council nominated, if Elizabeth should bear a son, as guardian to the child, if a daughter, as heir to his cousin's possessions. He thus, in name and claim, represented the Luxemburg line, although, strictly speaking, only very remotely connected with it; but as so representing it, he was the most obvious

candidate for the imperial succession, and, although he
did not put himself forward for it, his friends did. After
an offer of the crown to Lewis III. the Pacific, Landgrave
of Hesse, which was wisely refused, the whole of the
electors voted for the election of Frederick.

It is said that he took three months for consideration
before he vouchsafed to accept it, but of this it is
impossible to be sure. If he did, it is characteristic
enough; and perhaps he waited to see whether
Elizabeth's child would be a boy or a girl. The election
was made on February 2, 1440; on the 22nd the
little Ladislas was born to his two crowns, and yet
not until Whitsuntide did the slow Frederick appear at
Frankfort to complete the formalities of the succession.
He was not crowned at Aix-la-Chapelle until June 17,
1442. He was at the time of his election twenty-five
years old, and had made the pilgrimage to Jerusalem.
He was the son of Ernest of Hapsburg by Cymburga,
daughter of the Duke of Masovia, the lady who brought
into the imperial family the characteristic Austrian life,
·and whose strength is said to have been so great that
she could twist a horseshoe in her fingers. But from
this distinguished pair Frederick inherited very little
except his personal advantages.

The Hapsburg Lands. — The Hapsburg possessions
were at this time split up more widely than they had
ever been; for, under the earlier posterity of Rudolf and
Albert, they had been held by the princes of the house in
a sort of joint tenancy, which secured, as long as it lasted,
the unity of the widespread heritage, including Alsace,
and the Breisgau, the Swiss possessions of the Hapsburg
county, Tyrol, Carinthia, and Carniola, as well as Austria
itself. But in the year 1411 the domains had been
divided, and the Tyrol, Carinthia, and Austria proper

formed three several duchies. The duchy of Austria fell to Albert, afterwards emperor; Ernest and Frederick, his cousins, divided the rest. The portion of Ernest was Carinthia and Styria, and these countries at his death devolved on Frederick III. and his brother Albert. Frederick thus obtained the crown of Germany with only his half of Carinthia and Styria, and with the wardship of the little Ladislas, to live upon. Ladislas, of course, inherited Austria proper, as well as his mother's kingdoms; the Tyrol was still a separate county, and Albert of Carinthia retained claims over the portion of Ernest, not less strong than those of Frederick. Nor did Frederick ever obtain the whole command of the Austrian inheritance.

In 1457 Ladislas died, but his portion was divided between the emperor and the other two dukes. In 1463 Duke Albert of Carinthia died, and Frederick came in for his share individually, but it was not until 1492 that the Tyrolese branch became extinct, and then its possessions were handed over, not to Frederick, but to his son Maximilian. Frederick did not marry for territory. He waited for twelve years, after he became king, before he married, and then (in 1452) took a Portuguese princess, who was the mother of Maximilian.

The Councils.—The first point to be mentioned and dismissed is the conclusion of the struggle between the Council of Basel and the papacy. That council had been struggling, as you will remember, against the policy of Eugenius IV. from the moment that it had been, against his wishes, got together. The Councils of Florence and Ferrara, held by Eugenius during this period, although extremely interesting in themselves, do not concern Germany, and we cannot afford to do more than mention them. The Council of Basel sat in opposition all the time they were sitting; and, when Eugenius announced that he had united the Eastern and Western Churches at Florence, the Council of Basel determined to depose him. This was done in May 1439, before the death of Albert II., who, however, was too busily employed to interfere, had he wished; but the deposition was approved by his ambassadors as well as by those of France. Amadeus, Duke of Savoy, was elected some months after as Felix V. (October 28, 1439); and, almost coincidently with this election, Albert II. died (October 27).

Much as the supporters of the Council of Basel longed for reformation and detested Eugenius IV., they were not disposed to run any risks for Felix V. Germany especially was desirous not to burn her fingers with a schism. And the Diet of Mainz, before the election of Frederick III., had declared itself neutral; it would support the Church, but would take no part between Felix and Eugenius. Neither pope was strong enough to injure his rival temporally; the great powers of Europe took little interest in either. In three diets at Mainz, Nuremberg, and Frankfort, both parties were heard through their envoys, but no other decision was arrived at. And matters drifted on until the year 1445, when Eugenius, strengthened by the adhesion of Aragon and the pacification of some of his Italian enemies, ventured to depose the Archbishops of Cologne and Trèves as adherents of Felix. This measure compelled Frederick and the empire to take some action at last; that action was managed by Æneas Sylvius Piccolomini, afterwards Pope Pius II., one of the greatest men of the century, the subject of one of Milman's most entertaining chapters, and the hero of Creighton's two volumes. Æneas Sylvius had been secretary to the Council of Basel, afterwards to the anti-pope, and thirdly to Frederick III., who had crowned him, as his poet-laureate, with his own hands.

The Papacy.—A man of great power and consummate versatility, he had contented himself, since he had attached himself to Frederick, with letting things take their course. In 1445 he went as imperial ambassador to Rome, and began to draw the rival powers together; after his return, upon the violent proceedings of Eugenius against the archbishops, he joined the envoys of the electors in their negotiations, very secretly cognisant of the counsels of both parties, and bent all his energies towards a reconciliation, which he saw could be won only by the humiliation of the Council of Basel and its antipope. He was received by Eugenius IV., who listened to his proposals, and, on his departure from Germany, named him his secretary, so that he now stood in the same relation to both pope and emperor.

It is impossible to follow the slow progress of negotiations. By bribery and forgery, as Milman states it, by double-dealing and exceeding cleverness, according to Creighton, Æneas obtained the submission of Germany and the renunciation of the council. By bribery he divided the electoral body, and by a forgery he persuaded them that the pope had cancelled the deposition of the archbishops. His policy succeeded better than it deserved. Just as he brought the news to Rome, Eugenius died; his successor, Nicolas V. (Thomas Parentucelli of Sarzana), was sincerely desirous of peace, and, two years after his accession, in 1449, the Council of Basel broke up. Felix V. abdicated, and the struggles of the Church of Rome for unquestioned supremacy as against emperor and council were at an end.

Three years after the breaking up of the council Frederick went into Italy with his bride, Eleanor of Portugal, and at Rome, March 18, 1452, he was married and crowned by Nicolas V. On this occasion was ratified the concordat, agreed on before the death of Eugenius IV., by which the ecclesiastical affairs of Germany were regulated down to the eighteeenth century. The chief points of it are five: (1) the restoration of canonical election of the bishops by the chapters; (2) the abolition of provisions and expectatives; (3) the right of the pope to fill up benefices vacant by translation or by sentence of the holy see; (4) the pope to fill up vacant canonries one half of the year, the chapters the other half, (5) the commutation of Annates for a fixed payment by way of first-fruits.

Germany, Hungary, Bohemia.—During the whole of these years, 1440 to 1452, Germany and the neighbouring lands were full of war. In Switzerland the confederate cantons made war on Zürich, which had concluded an alliance, offensive and defensive, with Austria against them, and attempted to found a new league; and the war that followed lasted until 1447. In 1450 the alliance was dissolved, and peace restored by the mediation of the neutral princes of Germany. Hungary and Bohemia, during these years, had no sound peace. The Hungarians, in contempt of the rights of the unborn Ladislas, offered their crown to Ladislas III., King of Poland; and, even after the birth and coronation of the child, received Ladislas as king.

In the war between the partisans of the two Ladislases, Amurath II., Sultan of the Turks, invaded the kingdom. He was defeated by John Corvinus Hunyadi, and peace

N

was concluded; but it was immediately broken by Ladislas, who was defeated and killed in the fatal battle of Varna in 1444. His death left the throne open for Ladislas Posthumous; but Frederick had not the means of enforcing his rights, and would not give up either him or his crown to the Hungarians. John Hunyadi was declared regent, and he for eight years carried on an adventurous war against the Turks.

In 1453 Ladislas was sent to rule in Hungary, which he misgoverned for five years, Hunyadi's influence being despised by him, although his kingdom owed its very existence to his prowess. On the death of Ladislas in 1457, Matthias Corvinus, son of Hunyadi, was chosen king. Frederick, claiming Hungary as an escheat, declared war against him; but, as he had no means of carrying it on, Matthias invaded Austria, and occupied the whole country except Vienna itself. The emperor was forced to sue for peace. This uncomfortable relation between Austria and Hungary continued to subsist during the remainder of the reign. Frederick was too proud to concede all that Matthias wanted, and too poor to resist him. The result was that Austria was, as often as not, in the hands of the Hungarians, and the emperor an exile in the midst of his empire. Matthias died four years before Frederick, who even then failed to obtain the election of Hungary for Maximilian; and it was not until 1527 that the house of Austria, in the person of Ferdinand I., obtained the apostolic crown.

In Bohemia the emperor was no stronger than in Hungary, although there the struggle was complicated by religious and national influences. There the crown was early offered, as I have said, to Frederick, who refused it in order to maintain the rights of the little

king, and Ladislas obtained and retained the title without
a rival; but the whole power of Bohemia was engrossed
by George Podiebrad, who played the same part there
which John Hunyadi did in Hungary, and, on the death
of Ladislas, was elected as his successor.

George Podiebrad was not so successful as Matthias
Corvinus, except against the poor Frederick, who
suffered from both of them. George was, moreover,
a heretic, and the pope incited Matthias against him
with the promise of the crown. But on his death
in 1471, Ladislas, son of Casimir, King of Poland, by
Elizabeth, daughter of Albert II., succeeded by the will
of George. Both candidates compelled Frederick to
give them the investiture of Bohemia; and war between
them lasted until 1478, when they agreed that peace
should be made, and the provinces of Lausitz, Moravia,
and Silesia should belong to Matthias for life; and in
1490 Ladislas was elected to the Hungarian throne as
well. His daughter married Ferdinand I., and brought
the two crowns to the imperial house.

It is impossible to exaggerate the innocent insignificance of Frederick during these wars. It was
not that George Podiebrad and Matthias did not
care about him: if they would have let him alone,
no doubt he would have been too thankful; but
they tried to use him, to defend him, or to em-
barrass him just as if he were the king in the game
of chess, with very little power, but a great deal of
consequence. The position would have been ignominious if it had been of Frederick's own choosing;
but he had no power, or the means of getting it.
He was alternately petted and bullied by his competitors; alternately an exile and an emperor, but
throughout devoid of anything like the substance of

authority. If he had possessed an army he might have found an opportunity in Italy.

Italy.—At Milan, in 1447, Filippo Maria Visconti died, and with him the family which he represented. Divers claimants presented themselves; but Frederick, although the Milanese would gladly have received him, was unable, alone of the competitors, to make a stroke for the ducal crown; after waiting for two months for his assistance, they were obliged to give themselves up to Francisco Sforza, who had married a bastard daughter of Filippo Maria; and thus, from the weakness of the emperor, arose that long struggle about the Milanese which enters into almost every continental war down to the end of 1866, constituting so large a part of the history of Lewis XII., Charles V., Philip II., the war of the succession of Spain in the eighteenth century, and even of the Italian campaigns within our own memory.

The Year 1453, *and after.* — The year 1453, which followed that of Frederick's coronation, saw the end of the Byzantine empire, and should have armed Europe for a crusade for the deliverance of Constantinople, if not for the frustration of all further attempts on the part of the Turks to push their way into Europe. Some show of zeal in this direction was exhibited by both emperor and pope. During the three following years several diets were held for the purpose, but no definite action was agreed on, and no one approved himself as fitted for command. Pope Nicolas V. died in 1455, and his successor, Calixtus III., in 1458. The next pope was Æneas Sylvius as Pius II. The crusade was the darling object of the whole of his policy as pope; and, before he reached the pontifical throne, it was the great end of the papal administration which he guided.

John Hunyadi.—The emperor, still under the influence of Æneas, now threw himself zealously into the plan, but he was too weak to do anything just without Germany, and the German churchmen were too jealous of an agreement between pope and Cæsar to lend their aid. The death of Ladislas Posthumous, in 1457, left Frederick more helpless than ever; he lost the influence which his position as the guardian of the King of Bohemia and Hungary might have gained for him, and he had no chance of the succession to which the family compact of 1440 would have entitled, if he could have constrained the two nations, which Ladislas had nominally ruled, to accept him. Fortunately the defence of Christendom for the time had fallen into hands better able than Frederick's to conduct it: first into those of John Hunyadi, who commanded the Hungarian nobles, in spite of the dislike of the boy Ladislas and his minister, the Count Ulric of Cilli; and after his death, which happened in the year before that of Ladislas, into the hands of Matthias Corvinus.

To John Hunyadi belongs the glory of having successfully stemmed the barbarian invasion. The papal legate, John Capistran, was the preacher of the crusade; John Hunyadi was the general; the deliverance of Belgrade in 1456 from the besieging army of Amurath was the great exploit. It cost the Turks 40,000 men; and, in memory of it, the feast of the Transfiguration was raised in rank and solemnity by the pope, Calixtus III. A month after the battle Hunyadi died. Matthias Corvinus was hardly less heroic in this respect than his father. In 1463 he even made reprisals on the Turks, invaded Bosnia, and inflicted a very severe defeat upon them. In the following year he was less successful, and, for several years after, his energies were diverted

from the great task by his quarrels with George Podiebrad and with the emperor himself. In 1479 he found
himself sustaining the struggle single-handed with the
infidel: neither the pope, for the spirit of Pius II. had
vanished with him in 1464, nor the Venetians would
help him. Frederick was also employed in his own
estates, and rather inclined to hinder than to help him.
Matthias, however, was equal to the task; from 1479
to 1485 he, by a series of successful campaigns, wearied
out the invading armies, and, as soon as he had obtained
a lull, set himself to punish the unkindness and passive
hostility of the emperor.

The part taken by Germany and the empire in the
defence of Christendom is now apparent. The struggle
lasts from 1455 to 1485—thirty years—during which the
emperor's part was confined to an authorisation of the
Crusade, the battles of which were fought by Matthias
and his generals.

Frederick's Difficulties.—In all these events Frederick is simply conspicuous by his absence; nor,
except remotely, do these events affect the inner life
of Germany. It is needless to repeat that the country,
while kept externally at peace by the inactivity
of the emperor or his helplessness, was internally
harassed with constant bloodshed, and quarrels in-
numerable as they are unrememberable. Those which
concern the Austrian heritage are the ones in which we
should expect to see Frederick most active. The death
of Ladislas left the possession of Austria proper to be
contested by the agnates; the emperor himself, his
brother Albert, and Count Sigismund of Tyrol. Frederick, as emperor, was inclined to claim the whole;
Albert and Sigismund insisted on their shares; the
nobles of the country were willing to obey none of

the three. Albert took up arms against his brother,
and for six years, 1457 to 1463, the archdukes, for this
title had been bestowed on the whole family by Frederick
in 1453, set to the empire the good example of intestine
feuds. In these, as in everything else, Frederick was
unsuccessful; in all skirmishes victory declared for
Albert, and, but for the assistance of George Podiebrad,
Frederick would have lost Vienna, the last possession
that he retained.

In the year 1463 Albert died childless, and Frederick
gained his share by inheritance. Carinthia fell in the
reapportionment that followed the death of Ladislas to
the Archduke Sigismund, who retained it until in 1492
he resigned all to Maximilian, and was joined to the
Tyrol. From 1463 to 1477 Frederick retained his
Austrian possessions, in constant fear and dread of the
attacks of his neighbours. In the latter year he was
attacked by Matthias Corvinus, and only preserved his
territory by a humiliating peace, one of the terms of
which is said to have been the renunciation by the
emperor of his claims on Hungary; for six years this
peace and the occupation of Matthias in the Turkish
war gave him an uneasy security, although Matthias,
in constant raids, kept him on the *qui vive;* but in 1485
the evil day came. Matthias took Vienna and permanently occupied the greater part of Austria; even
Neustadt, the imperial residence, fell before him in 1486.
Frederick, with a retinue of 800 knights, went into exile
in the empire, canvassing the provinces, who cared
little for him, and summoning diets that cared scarcely
more. In 1487 he obtained succours from a diet
at Nuremberg. But Albert of Saxony, who was
placed in command of his force, preferred negotiation
to war with so powerful a prince as Matthias, and con-

cluded a truce with him, by which Austria was left in his hands until he should have recovered from the unhappy province all the expenses of the war. Such a truce meant nothing, except that there was to be no defence of Austria by Germany. The Hungarians remained in possession.

In 1489 the emperor again sued for peace. The negotiations hung fire until the next year, when Matthias died, still in possession of Vienna. Then the tide turned. Maximilian recovered his father's estates, and was able even to attack Hungary; but the disgrace remained; the Holy Roman emperor was not only unable to execute judgment and justice in the empire, was not only unable to conduct the defence of Christendom on the frontier, but was not even able to retain possession of the hereditary dominions of his house, or to rally the vassals to the defence of the integrity of the Fatherland.

It seems that Frederick's favourite maxim was *Rerum irrecuperabilium summa felicitas oblivio;* a proverb which might be Englished as "It is no use crying over spilled milk," and interpreted as recommending the virtue of resignation; but, literally translated, it can have no other meaning, than that the highest happiness is the forgetfulness of what is irrecoverable; a *summum bonum* cultivated, apparently, by him with as much zeal as he was capable of feeling for anything; and which the greatness of his losses as well as his talent for oblivion must have given him the greatest facilities for securing.

Maximilian.—In all this humiliation the only ray of cheerful light is to be found in the rising abilities of Maximilian, for whom, after considerable difficulties, his father succeeded in obtaining the crown of King of the

Romans in 1486. For him Frederick seems to have read the stars not altogether in vain. He is said to have invented the name for him, even the Christian name; a name compounded of those of his two favourite heroes, Quintus Fabius Maximus and Paulus Æmylius; but there is some doubt as to the truth of the story, and there is an inconvenient Maximilian somewhat earlier.

As he became free to take part in German politics his father's fortunes began to rise. Hitherto he had been an adventurer, so to speak. He had won, and lost by death before he was thirty, the heiress of Charles the Bold of Burgundy; and his work from that time had lain on the western side of Germany, in the defence of his children's inheritance. The growth of the Burgundian estates, and the greatest extent of the family power, the whole career of Charles the Bold, and his whole life except his seven years of childhood, fall within the limits of the reign of Frederick III. The aggrandisement of Burgundy at the expense of the Netherland cities, bishops, and nobles; the annexation on every side of the possessions of the empire to the dominion of one who, by birth, was a prince, and by tenure a vassal of the house of Valois, involved at every turn the dismemberment of what once was the German kingdom. And the same along the whole line of the frontier. Yet, grudgingly as the emperor must have viewed the aggrandisement of Burgundy, Charles was too much for him, just as Matthias Corvinus was.

In 1473, five years after Charles succeeded his father, he did homage to Frederick at Trèves for his Dutch dominions. But he demanded at the same time the title of king and vicar of the empire. Frederick was nowise loath, provided Charles would give his daughter to Maximilian: neither party trusted the other, and the project came to an end for Charles's life; but, shortly after his death, Maximilian married the heiress, and, after twelve years spent in securing her rights, was able to do something for his poor father. A little strength of any sort must have been a great change for Frederick, and he only survived the shock for three years!

Death of Frederick III., 1493.—Fifty years of absolute impotence and three of returning fortune make up the annals of his reign. He died on August 19, 1493, at the age of seventy-eight.

It is unfair to be critical about him; he never pretended to be a hero. We naturally compare him with Charles IV., but the comparison is favourable to Frederick. Both princes were great sticklers for imperial dignity, and neither had much of the substance of imperial power; but Frederick was a gentleman by nature, although an idle one; Charles was pretentious and eminently fussy. Neither Frederick nor Charles did anything great, or indeed did anything that was not extremely small; and yet both left the dominions and consequence of his house greatly increased. But Frederick never had the chance of doing anything great, and scrupulously avoided everything that was mean. Charles IV., on the other hand, stuck at no petty baseness, and was uninfluential because he chose to use his power, which as King of Bohemia was considerable, for the mere advancement of his family. Frederick's one scheme for the advancement of Maximilian did ultimately answer, but its success was due to the knight-errantry of the son rather than to the policy or the prowess of his father. The result is that Frederick had not the chances of Charles, or Charles the good qualities of Frederick; but then we have no guarantee for supposing that Frederick, with Charles's power, would have done more than he did, or that Charles, with Frederick's honesty, would have founded a greater dynasty, although he might have enjoyed a less disastrous reign. For the effect of it on Germany we must look forwards.

THE HOUSE OF HAPSBURG.

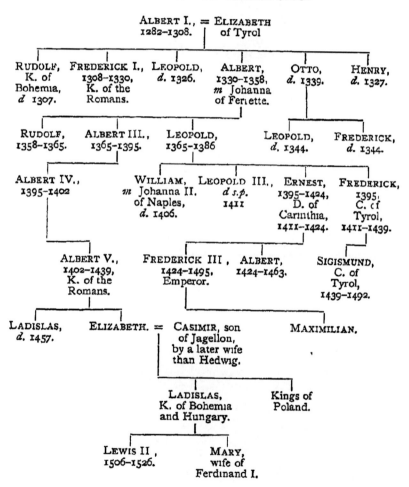

IMPORTANT DATES

Frederick III., 1440–1493.

Crowned Emperor at Rome, 1452.

Capture of Constantinople by the Turks, 1453.

Troubled Relations of Frederick with Bohemia and Hungary, 1457–1471.

Frederick meets Charles the Bold, 1473.

Marriage of Maximilian with Mary of Burgundy, 1477.

Treaty of Olmutz between Hungary and Bohemia, 1479.

Treaty of Presburg, 1491.

CHAPTER XI

Maximilian I.—Maximilian, the only son of Frederick III., had borne the title of King of the Romans for seven years before his father's death, and succeeded to the full status of his father, saving the imperial crown, immediately upon it; he was already crowned king, April 9, 1468, at Aix-la-Chapelle, and no further proceeding seems to have been taken to confirm the title. Maximilian was now thirty-four, and the most accomplished prince of his time, fond of warlike exercises, books, and music, but especially devoted to hunting.

As Frederick III. reminds us of Charles IV., so in Maximilian there is a trace of the character of Sigismund; again it is a higher type of character; but again the impoverishment of the imperial position renders the greater abilities in a great measure inoperative. There is very much of the adventurer, the knight-errant, even the troubadour, in Maximilian, but it is not let down, as in Sigismund, by pettiness and selfish policy. Maximilian is also, like his father, a somewhat, nay an extremely thriftless person, and therefore entitled to the sympathy and consideration of the thriftless generally. He was a greater European power than his father, and he had a more consolidated domain in Germany itself.

The acquisition of the Burgundian inheritance, even before he succeeded his father, placed him in the first rank of European princes; the death of his cousin, Sigismund of Tyrol, and his father's death three years later, placed him in possession of the whole property of the Hapsburgs; and in 1496, by the marriage of his son Philip, the heir of Burgundy, with the heiress of Spain—a marriage which placed him in the closest alliance with the strongest kings of Christendom, Spain and England—he found himself in a political position inferior to none of his predecessors.

It is unquestionable that his thriftless and adventurous character disabled him from making so much of his position as might have been made of it. But it is not to be forgotten that a political position, to be realised at all, must be based not only on titles and alliances, but on substantial wealth and power. The acquisition of the Netherlands did not supply wealth and power to Maximilian in any proportion to the political status that it seemed to give him. The death of his wife, in the early days of their married life, robbed him of the power that he would have had as her husband, and left him merely the guardian of his own son, a guardianship the exercise of which was limited on every side by the jealousy of the estates, and the profits of which were more strictly limited by reason and justice.

Rich as were the Flemish cities, they were not liberal to Maximilian, whom they regarded as a penniless adventurer; they required either pressure, which he was not strong enough to furnish, or that mutual good-will which was felt by and for Charles V., to draw the money from their purses. Maximilian fought their battles, but could not win their love.   His real strength then lay in his hereditary dominions, the long and varying strip of territory that extends from Alsace to the Hungarian frontier; which contains the whole of the Austrian estates accumulated by Rudolf of Hapsburg, with the addition of Carinthia and the Tyrol. This mountain territory, save that portion which was rapidly becoming Swiss, was thoroughly in hand under Maximilian, who indeed maintained his hold on Austria proper in perfect security; and the people of the states were enthusiastically attached to him; but they were the poorest parts of Europe, so far as money was concerned, and Maximilian had neither power nor will to act tyrannically.

In this respect, then, only, was he pecuniarily better off than his father; and, considering the actual work that he did, I think it may be allowed that he made more of it than might have been expected from his father's son.

The Imperial Position.—In considering the imperial position hitherto, we have traced it through three phases: in one the imperial demesne and status of emperor were regarded as self-supporting; such was the theory of the earlier emperors, much modified in practice, but still regarded as feasible, when taken in conjunction with the custom of hereditary succession.

But the squandering of the imperial demesnes by Philip of Swabia and Frederick II., and the advantage taken by the nobles and cities of the weakness of the kings who ruled or seemed to rule during the nominal interregnum, and whose authority was only recognised when it was used to impoverish the empire in favour of the vassal, had altogether changed the position of the emperor.   Instead of the demesne supporting him, it was necessary that he should be a prince with hereditary, organised dominions large enough to support imperial state and enforce imperial authority. For the credit of Germany he must be a German prince; although on several occasions English and French princes were put forward for the post, only on the double election of Richard and Alfonso were foreigners really chosen. Richard had wealth and territory outside the empire, nothing in it. Alfonso made no serious attempt to assert his claims except by words.

Under this second phase it was difficult to find a prince unwise enough or unselfish enough to waste his hereditary estates on the empire. It was simply this, as Lewis of Bavaria found it. To hold the empire at all it was necessary to drain his hereditary dominions, and, when they were drained, the result was beggary for himself and anarchy for Germany. The certainty of this it was that threw the empire for so long a period into the hands of the house of Luxemburg, and that went far to perpetuate it afterwards in the house of Austria.

As no adequately powerful German prince would ruin himself on the show of Cæsarship, it was allowed, and this is what I called the third phase, to fall into the hands of two successive houses which, although German, had besides their German territory very large non-German or semi-German possessions, by which the expense of the imperial dignity could be economised.

The king of half a dozen kingdoms need maintain but one court and household; the expenses of the court and household were, as is seen from English history, the most aggravating and oppressive drain on the subjects, who had very little money and knew no political economy; and, accordingly, if the empire were governed by a king who was also King of Hungary or Bohemia, or Spain or Burgundy, the dignity could be kept up at little expense to the empire itself. It found the majesty and dignity; the foreign kingdom bore a large share of the expense. Of course the result of this was, from the fourteenth century downwards, to direct the energies of the emperors, first as we have seen, to the extension of their hereditary estates, and, secondly, to the administration of them, to the neglect of the interests and of the administration of the empire at large; and hence arose anarchy at home and the paralysis of German influence abroad: anarchy finding its expression in private war, and developing its own corrective in volunteer combinations for the obtaining of justice; and a foreign policy which made the emperor occasionally the tool and hireling of contending powers, but never gave him room to be actually, as he claimed to be, an arbiter of quarrels.

In both respects Germany, under Frederick III., had reached the lowest rung of the ladder; and in both respects it is Maximilian's glory, whatever his faults may have been, and however far he fell short of his own or our ideal, to have taken steps that made a recurrence of such a state of things for the future impossible. It is true that the Germany of modern history is a different thing from the Germany of early medieval history, but there is at least more cohesion in it, from the reign of Maximilian downwards; I do not mean a more coherent organisation so much as a greater national feeling of unity, and that in spite of the introduction of entirely new elements of division by the Lutheran reformation.

Career of Maximilian before 1493. — The career of Maximilian, before his father's death, is soon told: he was born in 1453; well educated and trained by

O

Frederick, who was himself an accomplished man, and from whom Maximilian derived the great advantages of personal dignity and strength which fitted him for his rôle as knight-errant.

In 1477, at the age of twenty-four, he won his wife, Mary of Burgundy, and in 1482 he lost her; he learned the practice of war in defence of her possessions against Lewis XI. So early left a widower, he lost no time in looking out for another wife, and betrothed himself to the Duchess Anne of Brittany; and in faith of this alliance declined the offer of the queen dowager of Hungary, Beatrice of Naples, widow of Matthias Corvinus; a thriftless and characteristic proceeding, which the house of Luxemburg would not have been guilty of.

In his position as guardian of his son, the Archduke Philip, heir of Burgundy, he learned the temper of the Flemish citizens, and in 1488, being King of the Romans, was made acquainted with the details of prison life for several months at the hand of the men of Ghent. He was rescued by his father, who for once summoned energy, and prevailed on the Germans to make an effort for his son's deliverance. The next year he returned to Austria; in 1490 he recovered the possession of it on the death of Matthias Corvinus; in 1492 he obtained the succession to the Tyrol by the cession of Sigismund, who died in 1496; in 1493 he reconciled himself with Charles VIII., who had deprived him of his intended wife, Anne of Brittany, and with whom he had gone to war in consequence.

Emperor.—In that year he became sole King of the Romans and emperor elect. From the first he devoted himself to the correction of the state of anarchy and political impotency into which Germany had fallen.

But his first step was an unlucky one. He allied himself with Ludovico Maria Sforza, Duke of Milan, and married his niece, receiving with her 500,000 ducats, and in return investing Ludovico with the duchy, to the prejudice of the heir. This marriage, with a lady of so doubtful nobility and so unpopular character, was a disappointment to the German princes, and might have been a fatal one, dragging the empire once more into the vortex of Italian intrigues. It was, however, so far advantageous that it disabled Maximilian from taking part as a claimant in the quarrel for Milan, and his course with regard to it was, if not dignified, safe and comparatively honest.

The Diet of Worms, 1495.—It is, however, with the great diet of Worms in 1495, and in consequence of the need of supplies to counteract the successes of Charles VIII. in Italy, that the real interest of his reign begins, and from it flow the great measures of organisation, which constitute his title, the historical claim of Maximilian, to the gratitude of Germany. The great measures of the diet were (1) the establishment of public peace, and (2) the establishment of an imperial tribunal ;—the imperial chamber at Frankfort afterwards removed to Speyer, and later to Wetzlar, where it subsisted until 1806. These were supplemented later by two measures, which we will consider in conjunction with them, the establishment of the administration of circles in 1500, and that of the Aulic Council in 1501.

Two of these measures, the establishment of public peace and the administration of circles, had been attempted before ; the first several times, and both with some momentary success during the short reign of Albert II.

About each of these I shall say a few words at the risk of having to repeat what I have said before.

Proclamation of Public Peace.—I. The proclamation of the public peace was directed to the abolition of the practice of private war. Private war was one of the great curses not only of the feudal system but of the Teutonic system generally, and perhaps we may go deeper still, ascribing it to the necessary conditions of imperfect civilisation, corresponding in origin with the blood feud and vendetta. It was not peculiar to the feudal system; indeed, one of the best features of feudalism in its best estate was the check it put upon the practice, by furnishing in an appeal to the high justice of the Lord, a resource by which the use of arms might be dispensed with.

But in the decay of feudalism, when every vassal tried to be independent of his town and tyrant over his dependants, when the central power had by lavish privileges, or by its own inherent weakness, divested itself of any practical influence in the decision of the quarrels of the nobles; when, as in Germany, the emperor had ceased to be the feudal judge of his dependants, and the sentences of the diets were inoperative unless they found a champion to carry them out for private ends; the barbarous state of public peace returned, and every man, or at least every noble, claimed a right to redress his own wrongs in arms. In England we only had experience of this state of things under Stephen; it was remedied by Henry II. by the destruction of the castles of the barons, and by the diffusion of justice in central and provincial judicature; but in France it subsisted long and widely; and in Germany, notwithstanding the strong prohibitions of Henry III., even as early as the twelfth century it had become the normal state of things.

It was to limit the universal practice that Frederick Barbarossa granted to his princes the *jus diffidationis*, forbidding by law that any hostile measures should be begun, without a solemn declaration of war and three days' notice; all transgressors were to be regarded as mere robbers.

As so often happens, the attempt to limit an evil results in the licencing or legitimising of it up to the point at which it is limited; and increases the audacity of those who are beyond the limit. The law of the *jus diffidationis* was construed to have this effect; every one who was strong enough to wage war openly availed himself of it on every opportunity; and those who possessed fastnesses for refuge turned them into dens of robbers. The wars of the former were justified by the challenge; the exactions of the latter were made in spite of a law which it was not the province of any one to enforce.

This state of things it was which moved Frederick II. on the occasion of his second visit to Germany to proclaim the great peace and to attempt the foundation or restoration of an imperial court of justice. But neither he, Rudolf of Hapsburg, nor Charles IV., nor his successors were strong enough to enforce it, and the court itself scarcely continued to exist at all; nor was Frederick's attempted restriction of the *jus diffidationis* to cases where justice could not be obtained any more successful; no such enactment in the nature of things could be of use which left the determination whether or no justice had failed to the parties in the quarrel.

As the process of disruption went on, and the little remaining central authority became effete, the anarchy became chronic; the country was impoverished by the oppression of the nobles, and weakened by the sacrifice of blood and money on these quarrels, to an extent that, taken in conjunction with the want of political combination among the states, accounts for the insignificance of Germany in European politics, and for the fact of her kings and princes appearing in European wars only in the character of mercenaries. But as the disruptive process began, as it did in the fourteenth century, to give way to the accumulative, the need of a central jurisdiction impressed itself more on men's minds than before : and even the judicial journeys of Charles IV. were not without their good effect. As the greater princes, the electors especially, both secular and ecclesiastical, gained and consolidated larger territories, they were better able to secure peace and keep their vassals in order.

Those districts in which the process of consolidation was not going on, such as Swabia, the Rhine countries, and Westphalia, had recourse to voluntary associations ; those leagues, confederations, and societies, partly of an aristocratic character, like the military orders, and partly of a republican character, like the Swiss confederacies, with occasional Vehmic tribunals, of which I spoke in discussing Lewis of Bavaria and Charles IV. These leagues, sometimes of cities against nobles, sometimes of nobles against nobles ; sometimes of cities and nobles of one district against cities and nobles of another, became gradually known and welcome to the legal machinery of the empire ; and capable of definition and authorisation by imperial law. Albert II. has the credit of having first recognised them and legalised them as circles. In the diet of Nuremberg in 1438 he abolished all the existing feuds, and appointed a body of Austregas to decide quarrels of the sort that had issued in these challenges, in imitation, perhaps, of Frederick II.'s abortive design.

But Albert's early death left his design also abortive:
during Frederick III.'s reign it was often debated, but
never actually revived until 1486, when a ten years'
peace was proclaimed; and at last, in 1495, Maximilian
was strong enough, and the desire of Germany earnest
enough—for I believe the execution of the reform was
forced on him by the diet—to put an end for ever to
the evil. Peace was proclaimed, the law of defiance
abolished, and the imperial chamber instituted.

The Imperial Chamber.—This imperial chamber consisted of a supreme judge with sixteen assessors, named
by the emperor with the approval of the diet. Its functions
were, first to entertain appeals in private causes, all such
causes being, by the primitive law of Germany, common
to all the nations, begun in the national or provincial
courts, tried by the national law, and only referred to
the king in the last appeal; and secondly, to determine
disputes between the different states. But even this
latter was appellate jurisdiction only, the disputes being
carried in the first instance before a body of arbitrators
or Austregas, such as were nominated by Albert II.;
and coming before the imperial chamber only in the
shape of appeals. By this organisation of the imperial
chamber all causes such as had led to private war were
capable of determination, if the country possessed the
means of enforcing it. That means was found in the
legal organisation of the circles.

The Circles.—This, as I have said, was done by Albert II.
and, like the other, had to wait for its full development
until the diet of Worms in 1495. The first division into
circles in 1438 left out the domains of the emperor, and
comprised only four: (1) Bavaria and Franconia; (2) the
Rhine country and Alemannia; (3) Westphalia, and (4)
Saxony; subsequently Albert added two more by sepa-

rating Franconia from Bavaria, and Swabia from the Rhine lands. This arrangement was revived by Maximilian in 1501; and in 1512 he added four more; divided the Rhine into Upper and Lower; Saxony into Upper and Lower; and incorporating the imperial states, Austria as the circle of Austria, and the Netherlands as the circle of Burgundy. Prussia and Bohemia also were proposed to make up the dozen, but their representatives protested against it in fear of increased taxation.

The administration of the system of circles is a further point :—briefly, it contained an organisation for both war and peace. At the head of each circle stood two functionaries ; a director and a military commander : the director assembled the states and regulated the business ; the general administered the forces and commanded in war. One circle of Austria was administered by the emperor; Bavaria by the Duke and the Archbishop of Salzburg; Swabia by the Duke of Würtemberg, who, by-the-bye, reached the status of a duke in this great diet of Worms, and the Bishop of Constance; Franconia by the Burgrave of Nuremberg, of Bayreuth, or Culmbach, by the Bishop of Bamberg ; Upper Saxony by the Elector of Saxony; Lower Saxony by the Duke of Brunswick and the Elector of Brandenburg alternately with the Archbishop of Bremen ; Westphalia by the Bishop of Munster and the Elector of Brandenburg ; the Lower Rhine by the Elector Palatine and Archbishop of Mainz; the Upper Rhine by the same Elector and the Bishop of Worms. Burgundy, so long as it continued to be a circle, was administered by the duke, who was also King of Spain.

The circles were separately assessed by a tax or subsidy entitled the Roman months, being originally intended to furnish the emperor with a force of 20,000 foot and 4000 horse, to carry him to Rome for the imperial crown. The circle of Burgundy, originally assessed at the tax due from two electorates, was early excused, and the sum furnished from the circles proportionately reduced; it amounted in this shape to 75,840 florins in the eighteenth century.

The Diet.—Whilst speaking of these assemblies, it may be remarked that the constitution of the diet itself, which was not finally settled until 1580, contained three Colleges of States. The first was that of the seven electors; the second the princes of the empire, secular and ecclesiastical; and the third the imperial towns in two benches, Swabia and the Rhine.

It is not known when this arrangement became the rule, or how the nobles below the rank of prince were excluded, but it appears in full force early in the fourteenth century, and regularly downwards. The counts, who were not as princes members of the diet, but were immediately subject to the empire, were divided into four benches or classes, those of Wetterau, Swabia, Franconia, and Westphalia, and there was another class which claimed entire allodial independence, as far as tenure is concerned, the free counts and free barons of Swabia, Franconia, and the Rhine.

Justice.—It will be remembered that, so far as concerns the administration of justice, not by appellate jurisdiction, and after the extinction of the imperial jurisdiction exercised through *Comites Palatini* or *Pfalzgrafs*, every prince had the power and right of it in his own dominions. This was acquired at various times by separate grant or by general privilege from the emperor, and was not uniform throughout Germany: some princes having a higher and wider jurisdiction than others; but in general it covered everything except the right of appeal, and that could be exercised only in peaceful times and at great expense.

The Imperial Towns.—In all matters of the kind the imperial towns stood on the same footing as the princes. Such an organisation as the diet, from which the lower nobility, the most dangerous element, was excluded, might have formed the basis of a national parliament, and created or carried out a national policy; but the points on which, during the humiliation of the imperial character, Germany could be called on to act as one nation were so few, and the powers of the diet to interfere were so limited by the privileges of the several states, that little real business was carried out in the assemblies. They served, however, to keep alive the idea of national unity, and came into play as powerful machinery in the following centuries, when the awakening of thought and the love of abstract argument in a measure superseded the appeal to brute force.

The Aulic Council.—The other reformative measure of Maximilian is one that does not call for much discussion, the institution of the Aulic Council. This was done partly in 1501 and partly in 1512, in a diet at Trèves. It owed its origin to Maximilian's wish to preserve the right of the emperor to hear appeals and to exercise supreme jurisdiction, a right which the constitution of the imperial chamber, the nomination of whose members required the confirmation of the diet, might be thought to infringe; and its functions were co-ordinate with those of the imperial chamber, being appellate only, besides possessing authority in feudal and some other causes, also by way of appeal.

The Aulic Council was supposed to follow the person

of the emperor like the original courts of law in England, but seldom did so ; it consisted, in the first instance, of eight members nominated by the emperor, but was afterwards increased, and, after the division of the empire between the Catholic and Protestant powers, was composed of a president, a Catholic, a vice-chancellor appointed by the elector of Mainz, and nine counsellors of each religion. Its relation as an appellate court to the imperial chamber may be compared with the relation of the judicial committee of Privy Council in England, to the House of Lords in its character of a tribunal of appeal.

The idea of two supreme tribunals of appeal is puzzling to the lay mind, but lawyers manage to reconcile greater inconsistencies than these, and generally have at least two strings to their bow. Matters of appeal, however, arising within the imperial domain, would naturally be referred to the Aulic Council rather than to the imperial chamber ; its authority extended, moreover, into Italy, whilst that of the imperial chamber was confined to Germany.

Maximilian's Work.—In all these measures Maximilian is entitled to a great deal of credit. It is not so much that he showed any originality in devising them, for not one of them was new in principle even in Germany, and all had been tried in the other Teutonic or feudalised kingdoms in one shape or other. At the best, his plan was but the expansion and diffusion of the plan of Albert II., but he has the credit of having got it to work, of having abolished the evils which Albert's short reign was not able even to face, and which had been rampant for the fifty-three years that intervened between them. He availed himself in the working of all the existing material, and framed it into a practical machine. From henceforth, if the internal peace of Germany was disturbed by private wars, they were not waged because there was no other resource than force.

It is true, as every student of later history must know, that the web thus woven was of a slight texture indeed, strong enough to constrain the small states, but powerless against the strong ones; and that, even when the imperial rule was by no means merely nominal, the electors and greater princes were accustomed to wage war against one another, and even against the emperor himself. But, on the other hand, there are many questions arising between both states and families, in which the interests are so far from general, and the principles at stake so little important, that the majority of the counsellors of both the adversaries would content themselves with arbitration rather than risk the expense and fortune of war.

Such causes, such quarrels, and, when the advantage of such a system is once seen, most petty quarrels will be seen to fall into the same category, were in an increasing degree settled by the new tribunals, and, if not general peace, yet much greater social security ensued. The robber castles, which for centuries had defied the emperor and the princes, simply because in a state of anarchy no robber knight was too insignificant to be worth the patronage of a powerful neighbour, were now an impossibility; the free nobles submitted to the emperor, and became his liegemen; the empire resumed, what it had not for a long time even pretended to, the forms and fashions of a united body. Much of this, I think, is owing to the adroitness, the versatility, and the general disinterestedness of Maximilian's own character.

Switzerland.—One curious result I may mention here from the establishment of the imperial chamber, and of the circular administration, namely, the recognition of the independence of the Swiss confederation. I have said little or nothing about this body in the last chapter, because for the most part its condition shared the general character of the condition of Germany; anarchy and petty wars. But, ever since the dissolution of the league between Zürich and Austria in the early days of Frederick; during the growth of the Burgundian power, and the impotency of the imperial, the confederate cantons had been drawing closer and closer to France; and, although still parts of the German kingdom, meddling little if at all in the troubles of the state.

The great series of victories won by the Swiss at Granson, at Morat, and at Nancy, terminate with the death of Charles the Bold; a war caused by the possession of the Austrian rights in Alsace by the Duke of Burgundy, under an agreement with Count Sigismund, which Frederick had been too weak to forbid. But the immediate result of the national deliverance was simply to renew the internal jealousies and dissensions which overwhelmed Switzerland as well as Germany; and the history for the next five-and-twenty years consists of battles and intrigues, interesting only to the local antiquary.

About 1489 the states, princes, and cities of the Rhenish, Franconian, and Swabian district instituted a league, called in mockery the petticoat league, from the kilt worn by the nobles; but properly the league of St. George or St. George's Shield: it was one of the voluntary confederations I have been speaking of which were superseded by the administration of the circles. This league the confederate cantons refused to join, partly at the instigation, no doubt, of France, partly for fear of having their own organisation merged in that of the new association.

Although this spirit affected the cantons, it did not blind the imperial towns to the advantages of the alliance, and several of them joined. Bern was the head of the party faithful to the emperor and order, and opposed to France. In the diet of Worms, the Swiss were properly represented, and took part in the proceedings as members of the empire; but the jealousy of independence, which had been provoked by the Swabian league, was fanned into flame by French intrigue, and they refused to be bound by the arrangement of the circles with their taxation, or by the decisions of the imperial chamber.

It was, unfortunately, a favourite project of the emperor's most faithful subjects, the Tyrolese, to compel them to obedience; and whilst Maximilian was busy in the Netherlands in 1499, the Tyrolese invaded the Grisons. This led to a general contest, in which at last all the cantons were arrayed against Austrian dominion, and through it against the imperial rule. Battle after battle was lost. Maximilian himself was only prevented by the persuasions of his counsellors from rushing upon the fate of his father-in-law.

The Swabian war, short as it was important, was ended by a peace in September 1499, by which the emperor confirmed the confederate cantons in possession of their ancient rights and conquests, and ceded to them the administration of the Thurgau.

This was the last attempt of the house of Austria to recover their supposed or usurped rights in their native land, and also the last attempt of the empire to enforce obedience to its decrees. Henceforth Switzerland was independent, but it did not cease to be nominally a portion of the empire until the peace of Westphalia in 1648.

The external history of the league consists for the future of accretions on the side of Savoy and Italy, and consolidation of its relations with the few intervening districts embraced within its own outer boundary. In the seventeenth century the Grisons were overrun by Austria during the religious wars which affected the whole continent, but this is scarcely an exception to the general statement that practical independence of the mountain land was recognised in 1499.

One other subject is connected with this great diet of Worms of 1495. It was called for the purpose of creating a force to oppose the French on the one side and the Turks on the other. The French were just undertaking the Italian expedition which is understood to mark the transition from medieval to modern history.

Hostility of France and Germany.—With the close of the fifteenth century begins the ranking of the French against the empire, the irreconcilable jealousy between France and Germany which so colours later history. It is not an old feature of their relations. Between practical France and manageable Germany, throughout the medieval period, lay a broad debatable land, gradually escaping from German influences, but not yet openly occupied or usurped by France. It included the old Burgundian kingdoms, and Lorraine and the Netherlands; all nominally imperial.

It was the gathering up of this borderland under the French house of Burgundy, and the devolution of them on the German house of Hapsburg by Maximilian's marriage which made them no more a debatable land, but an actual bone of contention and prize of war. The two rivals are no longer separated by a territory narrow

enough to shake hands over, but too wide to fight across ;
they meet face to face ; the debatable land having been
Frenchified by Burgundian rule, and become German
by the Burgundian marriage is an anomaly in Europe,
that each side is anxious to do away with for its own
purposes. France herself also is nerved by her struggle
with Burgundy, for a struggle with the inheritors of
Burgundy. Such is the key to the history of Charles V.
The rest of Maximilian's reign belongs to later history.

IMPORTANT DATES

Expedition of Charles VIII. of France to Italy, 1494.
Diet of Worms, 1495.

CHAPTER XII

The Princes in Germany—The empire in abeyance—The real unity of Germany — The growth of the religious question — The characteristics of North and South Germany—The importance of the acquisition of the Netherlands to the Hapsburgs—The empire and France face to face.

The Princes.—It will not be difficult to arrange under several heads the various generalisations that we have arrived at. But before doing so it will, I think, be advisable to run briefly over the geographical aspect of Germany as we leave it at the end of the fifteenth century. We began in Chapter I. with the five dukedoms representing the ancient five nations still in existence, Saxony, Franconia, Bavaria, Swabia, and Lorraine; we leave them at the close of the fifteenth century so cut up, mutilated, recombined, that even where the old name continues we have no certain warrant that the country known by it contains an inch of the ground to which it was formerly applied.

Of the families, again, which we leave ruling the largest territories of Germany, scarcely a single one can trace its princely character so far back as the point at which we began, and some of the lay electorates had changed dynasties more than once during the time. The families, again, which have for two centuries held the imperial crown, have only rarely and accidentally possessed the electoral vote, the house of Austria notably, notwithstanding its extent of power and territory, did not, until the kingdom of Bohemia became permanently a part of its inheritance, acquire a direct voice in the election of the emperor.

As instance of the disruption of the ancient duchies we may take Swabia; this large territory, the duchy of which became extinct with the Hohenstaufens, had, under their lax and wasteful rule, become a prey to private war, robber counts, and a free nobility. Alsace was the only portion of it which continued to retain any unity, and that unity was not the result of internal causes so much as a consequence of the fact that the hereditary government belonged to a house otherwise strong. It was Rudolf of Hapsburg that consolidated the landgraviate or landvogtship of Alsace, and it was ruled by his descendants until the close of the period.

In Swabia proper the counts of Würtemberg rise early up to the surface as enterprising and unscrupulous chieftains in private war; their territorial advantages are improved between the thirteenth century and the sixteenth, and at the close of the fifteenth we find them raised to the rank of princes; a rank which, after three centuries more of pushing and struggling, was in the nineteenth century raised to royalty by Napoleon Bonaparte. The present kingdom of Wurtemberg roughly represents the ancient Swabia. But a better instance still is Saxony, a name still found on the map but not containing any portion, I believe, of the ancient Saxon land.

In the thirteenth century the ancient duchy which Henry the Lion had held is found divided between Cologne, Brunswick, and Brandenburg: the creation of the duchy of Brunswick by Frederick II. separated into two all that was left of the original Saxony; the northern part was reduced to the little duchy of Lauenburg, of which we have heard so much in recent times;

the southern was gradually lost in the hotch-potch of the Thuringian and Misnian inheritances. The margraviate or electorate of Brandenburg conveys its name to the several possessions of the house of Hohenzollern, we have a Margrave of Brandenburg Culmbach in the heart of Bavaria; Bavaria itself, after diverse sub-divisions, retains its integrity, but the Palatinate pedigree, the other branch of the house of Wittelsbach, throws up detached saplings in the remotest parts of Germany, and defies the memory to retain its involutions.

The Great German Families.—Germany, in a word, from being an aggregation of distinct nations, has become an aggregation of the domains of several great families, or great functionaries lay and ecclesiastical.

As to these families, the Wittelsbachs are the only one that retain a leading position throughout; and they, although at one time they possessed two and claimed three votes in the electoral college, give only two kings, one from each branch, Lewis of Bavaria, and Rupert the Count Palatine, to Germany. The electorate of Brandenburg, at the opening of the period, held, like Saxony, by the Ballenstadt house, passes first to the Bavarian, then to the Luxemburg, then to the Nuremberg or Hohenzollern houses. The original Ballenstadt house which held both Saxony and Brandenburg sinks into the obscurity from which it scarcely even in modern times emerges under the name of Anhalt. So the face of the map varies from reign to reign, and the dynastic history of Germany fills a book as large as the "Peerage."

The arrangements of the circles which was explained in the last chapter is an improvement on the plan of the electorates, because it covers the whole territory and is a return to the state of things out of which the electorates sprang. The great duchies of the twelfth century had split into small divisions, the best of these almost accidentally coinciding with the territories to which the electoral dignity was secured in the fourteenth. The electorates themselves then underwent the process of attenuation, only occasionally counteracted by the accumulation of new estates; power passed from them into houses of less rank but greater territory and energy, like the Luxemburgs and Hapsburgs; and under them the imperial policy was glad to secure order by substituting for the ancient worn-out instruments of central jurisdiction an organisation which owed its existence to the national longing for unity and order. It is true that the administration of the circles was but a feeble expedient, as results prove, but it was something, and took the place of entire and absolute incoherence.

Weakening of the Empire. — We look next, still geographically, at the outlying parts of the empire; those which are only partly German or altogether non-German. We see Italy entirely lost, and, if any part of it is to be recovered, it must be under a new title. We have traced, though by no means elaborately, the advance of the Swiss cantons to a practical independence which Maximilian was obliged to recognise, but which had existed for a century at least before his time. The old kingdom of Arles comes next, and the last fragment of it that remains, the county of Burgundy, and the towns that have not yet identified their interests with the Swiss confederates.

It is true that even under Frederick Barbarossa the imperial hold on Arles was a slight one; it was slighter

still when Henry VI. invested Richard Cœur de Lion
with a kingdom which entirely ignored his sway; and
the acquisition of Provence by a branch of the royal
family of France made the maintenance of even a
show of supremacy more difficult. It was under Adolf
of Nassau that we saw the Count of Burgundy openly
withdrawing his allegiance from the empire to give it
to France. But France was not yet bold enough to
take all.

Charles IV. was crowned King of Arles, although
all he was suffered to do as king was to confirm
the alienations of the powers which his predecessors
since the days of Conrad the Salic had been unable
to realise. The remains of the Burgundian kingdom
form a part of the new dynasty of Burgundian dukes,
which ends in the wife of Maximilian. And thus by a
curious revolution, and for a short time, they return to
the empire.

In something like the same way it has happened in
the Netherlands, which came round to the empire after
a similar long alienation. It is very long since we saw
the emperor exercising any authority in Holland or
Friesland. The house of Flanders, intensely French
as it has become, was not originally alien to the
empire. But it has grown, and spread French influence
as it grew, until the language of the states is more
French than German: it also is swallowed up in the
Burgundian heritage and comes back to Maximilian.
Last of all is Lorraine, which, the last possession of the
Karolings, the most bloodily contested of the battle-fields
under the Ottos and Henrys, although remaining German
in allegiance, has become French in alliances and connections, so much so that from the reformation downwards we count the Duke of Lorraine a Frenchman, and

forget that little more than a hundred years ago the county was still German.

On all these sides German influence and imperial authority have become second, either to French influence or the desire of independence. The burghers of Ghent and Antwerp had the same passion for freedom that inspired the Swiss confederates to their emancipation; and both would have gladly maintained the imperial authority against their mesne lords and oppressive neighbours, if they could have found and laid hold of the imperial authority to maintain it. But the Swiss relations to the empire were complicated by the claims of the Hapsburgs on their native territory, and the Flemish burghers forgot the existence of a central power which had forgotten them. In these remote regions the imperial rule had become like the feudal system in England, a matter interesting only to the legal antiquary or to the conveyancer proving the title and tenure of a disputed estate. The empire here was in abeyance.

To account for this abeyance would be to recount the whole history of the three centuries we have travelled over. It was not that the emperors were bad men or bad rulers: few countries have ever had such a succession of princes to whom the name of tyrant was less applicable; they were almost always wise, and brave, and kindly men. But they were, as a rule, poor, or if not poor to begin with, quickly impoverished by the demands of their position; and if they took the ready means to mend it, they lost their title to respect and any influence they might else have had.

Italy and the Empire.—Two things, however, we saw accounted for it still more fully. The innate incapacity for cohesion in the mass of distinct nations, each with its own princes, history, laws, and wars; and the action of the papacy: the latter acting in two ways—first, as it was affected by the claims of the emperor touching the Church; second, as it was affected by his claims, imperial or dynastic, touching Italian territory. The earlier disputes between the empire and the papacy arose from imperial questions; reformation in the Church, investitures, the exercise of imperial sovereignty. From the marriage of Henry VI. to the end of his dynasty, and even after it during the troubles of Lewis of Bavaria, the origin of the difficulties was the possession or claim to Italian territory. Even the popes when in exile in their Babylonish captivity at Avignon, far from Rome for half a century, would not tolerate the possession by German rulers of Italian soil. Unworthy as was their policy, actuated more by the promptings of France than by their love of Italy, it was very fatal to Germany; for it so weakened the imperial power as to render it unable to hold Germany in order much less to hold Italy in awe.

It was the relation of the papacy to Lewis of Bavaria that broke the remaining power which had survived the Hohenstaufen, had been nursed up into action by Rudolf and was exercised by Henry VII. That relation was created by the pressure of France exerted to secure the maintenance of her younger branch on the throne of Naples.

Well, indeed, may we say that Italy was a fatal gift to Germany: so fatal that all that Italy was doomed afterwards to bear from German hands counts but as an imperfect requital. It destroyed the hope of anything like union in Germany. It kept Germany broken up into parties until no party was strong enough to maintain central government or order, and that being done every man did what was right in his own eyes, and still more easily whatever wrong he chose.

Tendencies towards National Union.—With all these tendencies towards division and causes and occasions of disruption, there were other more penetrating, subtle, and lasting tendencies towards national union.

Of these tendencies one is represented by language. The German language is common to the whole of Germany, and in proportion as the dialects cease to be commonly, mutually intelligible, the common feeling decreases in its intensity. Although in North Germany the Platt Deutsch was unquestionably more generally used and over a greater area than at present, and South German or High German (Hoch Deutsch) has been for centuries increasing upon it, as the language of courts, literature, commerce, and the more enterprising and larger half of the people, we must not conclude that the distinction between the two forms of the language points to any deep distinction of race. Just as the low German has sunk into a dialect and been driven farther and farther north by the spread of high German education, the divergencies between the two forms of the language have become greater.

Influence of Language.—So far as I am aware the main features of distinction between them are apparent in the earliest written remains we have of each of them, and those features are developed and extended, only, in the modern forms. But it is to be remembered how very late are the most ancient specimens of written German, low or high ; and that we have not a syllable of either more ancient than the date of that conformation of Germany under the five nations which I used as a key to its early history.

If, then, high and low German have for a thousand years been diverging, and been driven asunder by national divisions during that period, and yet can hardly be said now to be mutually unintelligible, we are safe in concluding the distinction between them to be as we know from other reasons they are, tribal rather than national. And where the language is the same, and the distinctions tribal or dialectic, rather than national; these, whatever may be the differences of government, and however long it may be since the divergency began, form a substratum, a basis for the feeling of national unity.

From the beginning of medieval history, Germany, divided between the Saxon, the Bavarian, the Swabian, and the Frank, has had this element of unity more really than the kingdom of England. Saxon and Bavarian with a different history, laws, and political feelings, even with a different religion, are more nearly one than England and Wales, although the two latter have everything but language in common. And language, even in this rough sort of unity which I am supposing to exist between high and low German, is a subtle as well as an obvious element of unity. As the common language of Germany fenced off the outer world which was not German, it must have also assisted the spread of thought and ideas in the same dress throughout the whole territory, whatever were the political or even the deeper tribal divisions.

To continue, however, all the Teutonic-speaking lands, except England and Scandinavia, which were remote and long ago separated, 400 years before we have the earliest scrap of German writing, all the German-speaking lands were under one supreme rule, and that supreme rule was vested in the first of earthly rulers, the Roman emperor, elected king of the German nations, but sovereign of the world by right of the Cæsarship.

This *civis Romanus* sentiment, little as the imperial character of Germany might be estimated abroad, was an object of pride fondly nursed by the Germans themselves; and especially where it connected itself with the imperial cities and the commerce and civilisation which they represented,—an object of an honest pride: the feeling of nationality was, of course, strongest in the imperial cities, which had both closer relations to the emperor, and mixed more with the world outside of Germany. It is true, however, that all Germans in language and in relation to the empire were brethren at home and abroad: the traditions of the unity of the empire and manners, customs, forms of law and ways of thought long survived the reality of the single rule, but by surviving they showed that the national instinct was stronger than the political pressure had been which it survived or than that which was now insufficient to extinguish it.

Influence of Religion.—To the influence of language and imperial traditions we must add that of religion and the Church. Divided into several great nations and into countless small dynastic estates, each claiming independence of all the rest, Germany still during the Middle Ages remained ecclesiastically organised on the outlines of the ancient original ecclesiastical geography. The ecclesiastical divisions originally agreed only incidentally with the political ones, and as changes took place in both they were carried out irrespectively of one another, and increased the divergence. Many districts, the civil governments of which were completely independent of each other, were severally subject to the same ecclesiastical head. And the German bishoprics were very wide, the provinces enormous in extent.

Here, then, as in England, we have the pressure of Church unity in the sense only of Church organisation, forming an influence towards civil unity. The South of England was one Church under the Archbishop of Canterbury long before Wessex, Mercia, Kent, and East Anglia were one kingdom. So in Germany, the subjects of all the little potentates on the Rhine, divided politically by the rule and alliances of their masters, were one in the obedience of their bishops, as well as in language and as subjects of the great empire.

In connection with this I should say that the cohesion implied in this organisation was not merely superficial. The religious feeling of Germany was, as it is, a very distinct thing: ecclesiastically the attitude of the Church towards the papacy is very traceable throughout the history: it is very jealous, very independent in every dispute attaching itself to the emperor rather than to the pope, until, and sometimes even after spiritual terrors are added to ecclesiastical ones; and, deeper still, as no one now can visit at the present day France, Germany, and Italy consecutively without being struck by the difference of the forms in which the common religion expresses itself, a deeper study of the literature of the churches reveals a deeper distinction between the ideas of the three, even as touching the same truth. The tendency to a peculiar sort of mysticism—I mean nothing in disparagement by the use of the word—is very rarely characteristic of German thought; distinguishing it from the logical precision of the French, and from the penetrating, enthusiastic ardour of the better Italian mind.

Growth of National Feeling in Germany.—It is not within my scope now to point out the way in which this mysticism helped to lead on towards the reformation; it is enough that I mark it as a distinction over and above those of mere politics and geography, tending to isolate the German schools, and throw them in more closely on one another, in opposition to foreign ones. The national spirit grew largely after the institution in the fourteenth and fifteenth centuries of the universities in which all that served towards unity, national, scholastic, and religious, developed more largely than elsewhere.

In illustration of the way in which this acted, I may adduce the often-quoted fact that a German could pass from the service of one prince to that of another within Germany itself without any imputation of disloyalty. He was the subject of each in turn, but not in a way that affected the questions of patriotism or nationality. Germany was his country, were he Saxon or Bavarian, the subject of the Archduke of Austria or the subject of the Prince of Reuss Ebersdorf.

In the late changes in Germany we saw Baron Beust pass from the service of the King of Saxony to that of the Emperor Francis Joseph, and this in both military and civil offices has always been the case. Moral baseness in desertion of a benefactor would be regarded on moral grounds, but not unless there were such, on the head of duty to any particular province; Germany was ever the Fatherland. But this must not be exaggerated; it is more true and applicable to the later Middle Ages than to the earlier ones, in which there was a great deal more general interchange of learned and able men than there was later. The state of things which was common in the twelfth was becoming peculiar to Germany in the fifteenth century: *i.e.* the nationality made itself felt in this way when the common practice had become extinct.

There was nothing strange in England in the eleventh century in having German bishops, nor in the twelfth in having French ones: some of Henry II.'s counsellors were Italians, and several ministers of William the Good, King of Sicily, were Englishmen. But in the next century this ceased to be possible; each land supplied its own ministers, lay or ecclesiastical, notwithstanding the pope's efforts to thrust in Italians everywhere. But the feeling of nationality, felt in Germany not less than elsewhere, to the exclusion of aliens, did not affect the relations of the Saxons and Bavarians, or *vice versâ*.

In no way is the reality, however, of this unity shown more than in the way in which the Germans are, and from time immemorial, from the tenth century at least, been regarded by foreigners. Among themselves they might be Hessian cat or Swabian hound; as at home we have Essex calves and Hampshire hogs; but to the world they showed themselves Germans, subjects of the *Semper Augustus, cives Romani,* and so on. And the world believed it.

The Name Germany.—It is difficult to account quite satisfactorily for the appellations given to the wide country now known as Germany, but the appellation given to the inhabitants by each neighbour is one equally applicable to all. To the Italian they are all Tedeschi; to the French Alemannians, to the English Dutchmen or Germans.

I am not prepared to say exactly at what period these names became stereotyped; but probably the use of the word Tedeschi by the Italians is ancient; it represents the generic name of Teutones. In England, down at least to the Norman Conquest, the distinction between Saxon and Lorrainer was known, and the specific names properly applied. William of Malmesbury seems to distinguish between the Germans and the Teutones. It is under Frederick Barbarossa that the use of the French name Alemanni is given by English writers to the whole congeries.

The use of the word Alemanni and Alemannia by the French is easily explained: the Alemanni being the first non-Frank tribe of Germany with whom the Merovingians came in collision. The Franconians, whom they first conquered, were Franks like themselves, and their name supplied no distinctive appellation; Bavaria lay beyond, far away: the non-Frank tribes who struggled just beyond the Rhine were Alemanni, and Alemanni they continue to be to the present day.

The use of the name German in English is comparatively modern. In antiquity, as you perhaps know, it had two significations, the wide one comprising all that is now Germany, and a narrow one in which it belonged to two smaller districts, Germania, Prima and Secunda, the narrow provinces stretching along the west or left bank of the Rhine.

I cannot think that the application of the name to these two districts can have had much effect in determining the modern use of the word, although it may explain Malmesbury's distinction; for the term Germany was always recognised as the ancient name, and used on occasion as Gallia is of France and Britain of England and Scotland.

Until comparatively modern times, the name by which Germans were known in England was generally Dutch; and the language high or low Dutch. Since the accession of the Hanoverian dynasty, it has been regarded as more dignified to use the word German; and Dutch is relegated to what was once Holland and Hollandish or Flemish. In Germany itself the original term is universal, Deutschland, and Deutsch; the title of King of Germany was invented by Maximilian I., and was perhaps regarded even then as a bit of pedantry, such as not uncommonly affects titles of honour.

I do not think these are trifles to a student of history; if they are, it is astonishing how much a little attention paid to them serves to clear up more important matters. If the titles of Justinian prefixed to the "Institutions" are a key to the wars of his reign, and remind one of the order of his triumphs and defeats, why is it not the case with modern potentates? Hear the title of Charles V., and you may see that on each peg hangs a series of historical incidents: Charles V., D.G., elect Roman Kaiser, to all time increaser of the empire (Semper Augustus), King of Germany, Castille, Aragon, Leon, both Sicilies, and Jerusalem, Hungary, Bohemia, Dalmatia, Croatia, Slavonia, Navarre, Granada, Toledo, Valencia, Galicia, Majorca, Seville, Sardinia, Cordova, Corsica, Murcia, Leon, Algarve, Algeciras, Gibraltar, the Canary and Indian Isles, Terra Firma and the Ocean Sea.

I need not run through all the minor titles which begin with Archduke of Austria, Burgundy, and Brabant, and come down to Count of Mechlin; but I may remark that they do not omit the original title, humble as it was, of Count of Hapsburg and Kyburg, Landgrave of Alsace and Margrave of the Burgau. And in the same way the King of Prussia's style was an epitome of his history: Burgrave of Nuremberg, Count of Hohenzollern, Margrave and Elector of Brandenburg, last of all King of Prussia. It is generally explained, of course, as a piece of foolish pomposity, but if he that hears will hear, it contains an easily remembered abstract of the whole history of the great house.

The Germans One People.—The conclusion to which we were coming was, that from the time of Frederick Barbarossa the Germans ceased to be distinguished by foreign nations, on ordinary occasions, into Saxons, Bavarians, Swabians, and the like, and became in common Alemannians, Dutchmen, Germans, and Tedeschi. And thus external treatment, as well as the instincts of a common origin, taught them to regard themselves as intrinsically one people, notwithstanding the enmities and different origins of their rulers.

We have now brought down our study of German history to the eve of that great event which for good or for evil, or for an altered mixture of good and evil, changed the complexion of Christendom, and the attitude of all the states of Europe one towards another. In none of these was the work of the reformation more marked than in Germany. In none was it more called for by ancient abuses, and in none was it carried to greater extremes.

The great restorative effort made by the Roman Church after the Council of Trent recovered much of the ground that had seemed to be lost, and the result in the seventeenth century was very much marked on the old lines of the nations. Lutheranism won the North, the ancient Saxony; the Roman Church retained a firm hold on Austria and Bavaria; Calvinism, the French form of the reformation, affected the Palatinate and the Rhineland. Switzerland furnished her own reformation in Zwingli; but the various divisions of Switzerland marked their nationality still by adhesion or opposition to the other forms of belief now marshalled against one another. Geneva, looking towards France, was the head of Calvinism; Basel and Bern, German towns, more especially were Lutheran; Zurich was Zwinglian; half the whole confederation, the half originally most bound up with Austria, retained the forms of the ancient faith. But not to insist on the minutiæ of this division, one cannot fail to be struck with the fact that North Germany, which had in all the contests between pope and emperor ranged itself on the side of the pope, now in this new division threw itself heart and soul into Protestantism.

The South of Germany, which had maintained the Hohenstaufen and their principles so long against the popes, is now found faithful. Of course, a multitude of other causes contributed to the result besides the religious ones, besides the political ones, and besides the tribal or even national antipathies of North and South. Of course, in a great measure the people were led by their rulers; the ecclesiastical provinces, with some great exceptions, remaining Catholic; the Saxons and the Palatinate following their electors.

But considering all these things, there is a residue that cannot be accounted for otherwise than as a result of the political training of ages. North Germany was more energetic and more in earnest than South. It was more religious, and had been from the very days of the Saxon conversion. It was less amenable to imperial influences, as we have seen in the last reigns that we have been considering. Yet we may conclude not unnaturally that if Charles V. had embraced the reformation, all Germany would have been to this day Protestant, or the North would have continued Catholic. The latter might have been the case, but considering the Saxon origin of Lutheranism, the former is the more probable.

In conclusion, then, let us sum up the moral of the

Q

history that we have traversed. We have seen in the three centuries between Frederick II. and Maximilian, a complete revolution in the relations of the empire with the papacy, and of North Germany to South. We have traced the imperial power in its variations from the perilous exaltation of Frederick, through his unparalleled humiliation, through the contemptible position of William of Holland and Richard of England, to the moment when Rudolf of Hapsburg restored it on quite another principle to something like majesty and power.

In the fifteenth century we have traced over again a similar revolution; from the actual zenith of power, as it was exercised by Henry VII., through the humiliation of Lewis of Bavaria, to the restoration of order and peace under Charles IV. But the revolutions of the fourteenth pale beside those of the thirteenth. Henry VII.'s power looks small beside that of Frederick II., and the fall of Frederick is not so abject as that of Lewis of Bavaria. The reinvigoration by Charles IV. is but an artificial affair compared with the resurrection under Rudolf of Hapsburg.

In all the events of the fourteenth century to the time of the great schism, we see the papal power, even in its greatest temporal weakness, gaining great ecclesiastical advantages. The schism paralysed it; but there was no king in Europe strong enough at the time to take advantage of the opportunity to set things right. Nor was there any state in Europe—I cannot except even the empire under Sigismund—strong enough in itself to take the lead in a determined reformation such as might have prevented or modified the evils which on any showing resulted from and thoroughly pervaded the reformation of the sixteenth century. The increase of the power of France in the fifteenth century went a long way to make a general reformation of the Church impossible.

The Advance of the Hapsburgs.—But, after all, and all things considered, it was the acquisition by the Hapsburgs of the Netherlands and Spain that changed the old form of things, and altered the whole face of European policy. France no longer looked at Germany over the Rhine and its broad borderlands, but wherever she looked, across the Pyrenees, across the Alps, across the Rhine, across the Meuse, in Spain, in Italy, in Germany, in the Netherlands, there she saw the same everlasting Hapsburg eagles. England, in spite of the reformation, maintained her alliance with the Hapsburgs; her instincts were German, and her antipathies were anti-French. As the Hapsburgs divided and grew weak, England sought new allies among the younger powers; but in all the great struggles of Europe she has had Germany, whether Austrian or Prussian, on her side. These things lie far before us. It is enough to say now that there is no country in Europe in which the medieval and the modern are more distinctly sundered from one another than they are in Germany.

INDEX

THE END

Printed by BALLANTYNE, HANSON & CO.
Edinburgh & London

Lightning Source UK Ltd.
Milton Keynes UK
UKOW021945120312

188825UK00008B/102/P